Café favourites

THE AUSTRALIAN Women's Weekly

DANISH

croissant

chocolate croissant   3

almond croissant   3

basil

danish - pear, apricot,   3·5
          raspberry

almond brioche   3·5

berry muffin   3·5

friand / palmier   2·5

doughnut - jam, custard   3·5

dough knot   2

AFTERNOON

chai brûlée tart   4·5

chocolate eclair   4·5

choc-raspberry tart   4·5

paris brest   4·5

grand marnier profiterole   4·5

fruit frangipane   5·50/2

berry custard tart   4·50/2

flourless orange cake   5·80/2

caramelised lemon tart   5·50/2

chocolate cake   5·80/2

contents

When making *Café Favourites*, we wanted to forget about low fat and fast, just for a little while, and focus on the food we crave. Modern food isn't about sticking to old notions of what we should eat and when, so this book is packed with recipes for the sort of food we can eat any time of day. My favourite part of the book has to be the sweets, with all the café classics like brownies and portuguese custard tarts: perfect for guests who just drop in. Cook café food at home and cure your cravings any time you like.

Pamela Clark
Food Director

café culture

Café food is comforting and tasty, familiar and welcoming. It defies cuisine pigeon holes – there are influences from Italy, France, America, the Middle East, Asia and the Mediterranean. The single qualifying factor for café food is that it must be delicious: the sort of thing you feel like eating any time of day. Now you can replicate this style of cooking at home. These days we're just as likely to have a salad, soup or toasted sandwich for dinner as we are a traditional meal. The food we eat in cafés is the epitome of this style of eating, and that's just the sort of recipes you'll find in this book. Light-as-air frittata or crispy salt and pepper squid for dinner is easy, and no longer do home-cooked breakfasts need to be confined to scrambled eggs on toast: for

a weekend indulgence make something special like strawberries and cream on brioche or corn fritters with cucumber salad. Sweet café classics such as portuguese custard tarts, friands and sticky date pudding can now be eaten fresh with that just-from-the-oven warmth. Café food is perfect for entertaining. It can easily be made in large batches or prepared in advance and finished off when you're ready to serve. Finger food such as dips, pizza for one, mini pies and refreshing drinks make pleasing a crowd a simple job. Lamingtons, scones and cookies are an irresistible treat for guests that just drop in. All your favourites are here, so you'll be able to enjoy them at any time of the day – no matter what you're craving.

preparation time 10 minutes | cooking time 5 minutes | serves 4

BLT on croissant

We used rindless shortcut bacon here, but you can use trimmed bacon rashers if you prefer.

12 slices rindless shortcut bacon (420g)
4 large croissants (320g)
2 small tomatoes (180g), sliced thinly
8 large butter lettuce leaves
aïoli
½ cup (150g) mayonnaise
1 clove garlic, crushed
1 tablespoon finely chopped
    fresh flat-leaf parsley

1 Preheat grill.
2 Cook bacon in large frying pan until crisp.
3 Meanwhile, make aïoli.
4 Toast croissants under grill about 30 seconds. Split croissants in half; spread aïoli over one half of each croissant then top with bacon, tomato, lettuce and remaining croissant half.
aïoli Combine ingredients in small bowl.
nutritional count per serving *36.8g total fat (13.9g saturated fat); 2592kJ (620 cal); 39.5g carbohydrate; 31.4g protein; 3.8g fibre*

fetta, avocado and roasted tomato toastie

8 x 1cm-thick slices walnut bread, toasted
250g fetta cheese, crumbled
30g baby rocket leaves
1 medium avocado (250g), sliced thinly
roasted tomato
2 tablespoons balsamic vinegar
2 tablespoons olive oil
2 cloves garlic, crushed
8 medium egg tomatoes (600g), halved

1 Make roasted tomato.
2 Top toast with cheese, rocket, roasted tomato and avocado then drizzle with pan juices.
roasted tomato Preheat oven to 240°C/220°C fan-forced. Combine vinegar, oil and garlic in small bowl. Place tomatoes, cut-side up, in medium baking dish; drizzle with vinegar mixture. Roast about 25 minutes.
nutritional count per serving *41.5g total fat (13.8g saturated fat); 2546kJ (609 cal); 37.1g carbohydrate; 19.5g protein; 6.2g fibre*

preparation time 10 minutes | cooking time 10 minutes | serves 4

huevos rancheros

"Ranch-style eggs" is a Mexican standard that has become popular all over the world. For an extra bite, serve with Tabasco, a fiery sauce made from hot red chillies.

3 chorizo sausages (500g), sliced thickly
8 eggs
½ cup (125ml) cream
20g butter
4 x 15cm flour tortillas
1 cup (120g) coarsely grated cheddar cheese
fresh tomato salsa
2 small tomatoes (180g), chopped finely
½ small red onion (50g), chopped finely
1 tablespoon red wine vinegar
1 tablespoon olive oil
¼ cup coarsely chopped fresh coriander

1 Preheat oven to 160°C/140°C fan-forced.
2 Make fresh tomato salsa.
3 Cook chorizo on heated oiled grill plate (or grill or barbecue) until well browned. Drain on absorbent paper; cover to keep warm.
4 Whisk eggs and cream in medium bowl. Melt butter in medium frying pan; cook egg mixture over low heat, stirring gently, until creamy.
5 Meanwhile, place tortillas on oven tray, sprinkle with cheese; warm in oven until cheese melts.
6 Divide tortillas among serving plates; top with egg, chorizo and salsa.

fresh tomato salsa Combine tomatoes, onion, vinegar and oil in small bowl; cover, stand 15 minutes. Stir in coriander just before serving.

nutritional count per serving *81.7g total fat (35.8g saturated fat); 4126kJ (987 cal); 16.2g carbohydrate; 48.2g protein; 1.9g fibre*

preparation time 10 minutes (plus refrigeration time) | serves 6

bircher muesli

2 cups (180g) rolled oats
1¼ cups (310ml) apple juice
1 cup (280g) yogurt
2 medium green-skinned apples (300g)
¼ cup (35g) roasted slivered almonds
¼ cup (40g) dried currants
¼ cup (20g) toasted shredded coconut
1 teaspoon ground cinnamon
½ cup (140g) yogurt, extra

1   Combine oats, juice and yogurt in medium bowl.
Cover; refrigerate overnight.
2   Peel, core and coarsely grate one apple; stir
into oat mixture with nuts, currants, coconut
and cinnamon.
3   Core and thinly slice remaining apple. Serve
muesli topped with extra yogurt and apple slices.
nutritional count per serving *9.2g total fat*
(3g saturated fat); 1120kJ (268 cal);
36.1g carbohydrate; 8.1g protein; 3.9g fibre

preparation time 10 minutes | cooking time 10 minutes | serves 6

strawberries and cream on brioche

3 eggs
⅓ cup (80ml) milk
1 teaspoon vanilla extract
1 tablespoon caster sugar
6 small brioche (600g), halved
40g unsalted butter
250g strawberries, sliced thinly
⅔ cup (160ml) thickened cream

1 Combine eggs, milk, extract and sugar in large shallow bowl. Submerge brioche in egg mixture.
2 Melt half the butter in large frying pan; cook half the brioche until browned both sides. Remove from pan; cover to keep warm. Repeat with remaining butter and brioche. Serve brioche with strawberries and cream.

nutritional count per serving *30.5g total fat (16.5g saturated fat); 2286kJ (547 cal); 53.5g carbohydrate; 13.4g protein; 2.8g fibre*

preparation time 10 minutes | cooking time 25 minutes | serves 6

blueberry buttermilk pancakes with bacon

2 cups (300g) self-raising flour
¼ cup (55g) caster sugar
2 eggs
600ml buttermilk
50g butter, melted
1 cup (150g) fresh blueberries
cooking-oil spray
12 thin rindless bacon rashers (360g)
½ cup (125ml) maple syrup

1 Sift flour and sugar into large bowl. Whisk eggs, buttermilk and butter in large jug. Gradually whisk egg mixture into flour mixture until smooth. Stir in berries, pour batter into large jug.

2 Spray large heavy-based frying pan with cooking oil. Pour ¼-cup batter for each pancake into heated pan (you can cook four at a time). Cook pancakes until bubbles appear on the surface; turn, brown other side. Cover to keep warm.

3 Repeat process using cooking oil and remaining batter, wiping out pan between batches, to make 14 more pancakes.

4 Meanwhile, heat oiled large frying pan; cook bacon until crisp. Drizzle pancakes with syrup, serve with bacon.

nutritional count per serving *15.4g total fat (7.7g saturated fat); 2224kJ (532 cal); 71.8g carbohydrate; 24.5g protein; 2.4g fibre*

preparation time 10 minutes | cooking time 20 minutes | serves 4

herb omelette with sautéed mushrooms

2 tablespoons finely chopped
   fresh flat-leaf parsley
2 tablespoons finely chopped fresh chervil
2 tablespoons finely chopped fresh chives
2 tablespoons finely chopped fresh tarragon
50g butter
2 tablespoons olive oil
250g swiss brown mushrooms, halved
½ cup (125ml) water
2 teaspoons finely grated lemon rind
1 tablespoon lemon juice
12 eggs

1 Combine herbs in small bowl.
2 Heat 30g of the butter and 1 tablespoon of the oil in large deep frying pan. Add mushrooms; cook, stirring, 5 minutes. Stir in 2 tablespoons of the water; cook, stirring, until water evaporates and mushrooms are tender. Remove from heat; stir in rind, juice and 2 tablespoons of the herb mixture. Cover to keep warm.
3 Gently whisk eggs and remaining water in a large bowl, whisk in remaining herb mixture.
4 Heat a quarter of the remaining butter and 1 teaspoon of the remaining oil in medium frying pan. When butter mixture bubbles, pour a quarter of the egg mixture into pan; cook over medium heat, tilting pan, until egg is almost set. Tilt pan backwards; fold omelette in half. Cook 30 seconds then slide onto serving plate.
5 Repeat process with remaining butter, oil and egg mixture, wiping out pan before each addition to make a total of 4 omelettes. Serve omelettes topped with sautéed mushrooms.

nutritional count per serving *35.3g total fat (12.9g saturated fat); 1714kJ (410 cal); 1g carbohydrate; 22.4g protein; 1.8g fibre*

preparation time 10 minutes | cooking time 20 minutes | serves 4

italian egg, prosciutto and cheese roll

4 eggs
4 focaccia rolls (440g), split
120g taleggio or fontina cheese, sliced thinly
4 slices (60g) prosciutto
8 large fresh basil leaves
tomato sauce
400g can crushed tomatoes
¼ cup (60ml) red wine vinegar
2 tablespoons brown sugar

1 Make tomato sauce.
2 Preheat grill.
3 Fry eggs in heated oiled medium frying pan until cooked as you like.
4 Spread bottom half of each roll with about one tablespoon of the tomato sauce; place on oven tray. Layer cheese and prosciutto on rolls; grill until cheese starts to melt. Top each with 2 basil leaves, an egg and remaining tomato sauce; top with remaining roll half.

tomato sauce Combine undrained tomatoes with remaining ingredients in medium saucepan; bring to the boil. Reduce heat; simmer 15 minutes.

nutritional count per serving *20.3g total fat (9g saturated fat); 2245kJ (537 cal); 58.8g carbohydrate; 27.5g protein; 4.1g fibre*

preparation time 5 minutes | serves 4

ricotta and banana toasts

8 x 1cm-thick slices fruit bread, toasted
1 cup (240g) ricotta cheese
2 large bananas (460g), sliced thickly
2 tablespoons honey

1 Top toast with cheese and banana; drizzle with honey.

nutritional count per serving *10.7g total fat (5g saturated fat); 2199kJ (526 cal); 87.1g carbohydrate; 15.8g protein; 6.6g fibre*

eggs and smoked salmon on blini

8 eggs
200g sliced smoked salmon
2 tablespoons sour cream
1 tablespoon coarsely chopped fresh chives
blini
⅓ cup (50g) buckwheat flour
2 tablespoons plain flour
1 teaspoon baking powder
1 egg
½ cup (125ml) buttermilk
30g butter, melted

1 Make blini.

2 Half-fill a large frying pan with water; bring to the boil. Break 1 egg into cup then slide into pan. Working quickly, repeat process with 3 more eggs. When all 4 eggs are in pan, return water to the boil. Cover pan, turn off heat; stand about 4 minutes or until a light film of white sets over each yolk. Using a slotted spoon, remove eggs one at a time from pan; place spoon on absorbent-paper-lined saucer to blot up poaching liquid. Repeat process to poach remaining 4 eggs.

3 Serve blini topped with eggs, salmon, sour cream and chives.

blini Sift flours and baking powder into medium bowl; gradually whisk in combined egg and buttermilk until mixture is smooth. Stir in butter. Cook blini, in batches, by dropping 1 tablespoon of the batter into heated oiled large frying pan. Cook blini until browned both sides; you will have 12 blini. Cover to keep warm.

nutritional count per serving 25.9g total fat (11.3g saturated fat); 1731kJ (414 cal); 14.1g carbohydrate; 31.5g protein; 1.6g fibre

preparation time 10 minutes (plus standing time) | cooking time 2 hours 45 minutes | serves 6

breakfast beans on sourdough toast

2 cups (400g) dried cannellini beans
1 tablespoon olive oil
1 large brown onion (200g), chopped coarsely
2 cloves garlic, sliced thinly
2 rindless bacon rashers (130g),
    chopped coarsely
2 tablespoons brown sugar
¼ cup (60ml) maple syrup
1 tablespoon dijon mustard
400g can chopped tomatoes
1 litre (4 cups) water
6 x 1cm-thick slices sourdough bread
2 tablespoons coarsely chopped
    fresh flat-leaf parsley

1   Place beans in large bowl, cover with water; stand overnight, drain. Rinse under cold water, drain.
2   Heat oil in large saucepan, add onion, garlic and bacon; cook, stirring, until onion softens. Stir in beans, sugar, syrup and mustard. Add undrained tomatoes and the water; bring to the boil. Reduce heat; simmer, covered, about 2 hours or until beans are tender.
3   Uncover; cook, stirring occasionally, about 30 minutes or until mixture thickens. Serve beans on toasted sourdough bread; sprinkle with parsley.
nutritional count per serving *6.3g total fat (1.1g saturated fat); 1626kJ (389 cal); 53.1g carbohydrate; 22.2g protein; 14.5g fibre*

preparation time 20 minutes | cooking time 20 minutes | serves 6

corn fritters with cucumber salad

You need to buy two large cobs of corn for this recipe.

1 cup (150g) self-raising flour
½ teaspoon bicarbonate of soda
1 teaspoon ground cumin
¾ cup (180ml) milk
2 eggs, separated
2 cups (330g) fresh corn kernels
2 green onions, sliced thinly
2 tablespoons finely chopped fresh coriander
cucumber salad
2 lebanese cucumbers (260g), sliced thinly
1 small red onion (100g), sliced thinly
1 fresh long red chilli, sliced thinly
⅓ cup loosely packed fresh coriander leaves
2 tablespoons sweet chilli sauce
1 tablespoon fish sauce
1 tablespoon lime juice

1 Sift flour, soda and cumin into medium bowl. Gradually whisk in milk and egg yolks until batter is smooth.

2 Beat egg whites in small bowl with electric mixer until soft peaks form. Stir corn, onion and coriander into batter; fold in egg whites.

3 Pour 2 tablespoons of the batter into heated oiled large frying pan; using metal spatula, spread batter into round shape. Cook, about 2 minutes each side or until fritter is cooked through. Remove from pan; cover to keep warm. Repeat process, wiping out pan between batches and oiling if necessary, to make a total of 18 fritters.

4 Meanwhile, make cucumber salad. Serve fritters topped with salad.

cucumber salad Combine cucumber, onion, chilli and coriander in medium bowl. Combine remaining ingredients in screw-top jar; shake well, drizzle over cucumber mixture.

nutritional count per serving *4.2g total fat (1.5g saturated fat); 882kJ (211 cal); 31.8g carbohydrate; 9g protein; 4.7g fibre*

preparation time 20 minutes (plus cooling time) | cooking time 30 minutes | serves 6

egg and cheese tartlets with capsicum relish

Balsamic white vinegar is a clear and lighter version of balsamic vinegar; it has a fresh, sweet clean taste, and is available from major supermarkets and good delicatessens.

2 sheets ready-rolled puff pastry
2 teaspoons olive oil
2 shallots (50g), sliced thinly
4 eggs
¼ cup (60ml) cream
½ cup (40g) finely grated parmesan cheese
30g baby rocket leaves
capsicum relish
1 tablespoon olive oil
1 small red onion (100g), sliced thinly
2 medium red capsicum (400g), sliced thinly
⅓ cup (80ml) white balsamic vinegar
2 tablespoons brown sugar
½ cup (125ml) water

1 Preheat oven to 220°C/200°C fan-forced. Oil a six-hole (¾-cup/180ml) texas muffin pan.
2 Cut pastry sheets in half; cut halves into three rectangles. Overlap two rectangles to form cross shapes; push gently into pan holes to cover bases and sides. Prick bases with fork, cover with baking paper; fill with dried beans or uncooked rice.

3 Bake pastry cases 10 minutes. Remove paper and beans carefully from pan holes; return to oven, bake about 5 minutes or until browned lightly. Cool pastry cases in pan. Reduce oven to 200°C/180°C fan-forced.
4 Meanwhile, make capsicum relish.
5 Heat oil in small frying pan. Add shallot; cook until soft.
6 Whisk eggs and cream in medium bowl; mix in cheese and shallots. Fill pastry cases with egg mixture. Bake about 15 minutes or until set.
7 Serve tartlets with relish and rocket.
capsicum relish Heat oil in large frying pan. Add onion and capsicum; cook about 10 minutes or until vegetables are soft. Add vinegar, sugar and the water; cook, stirring occasionally, about 15 minutes or until mixture thickens slightly.
nutritional count per serving *27.3g total fat (12.7g saturated fat); 1697kJ (406 cal); 28g carbohydrate; 11.7g protein; 1.7g fibre*

preparation time 20 minutes (plus refrigeration time) | cooking time 10 minutes | serves 6

asian-spiced fruit salad

You need two passionfruits for this recipe.

1 cup (250ml) water
1 tablespoon grated palm sugar
2cm piece fresh ginger (10g), grated
1 star anise
1 small pineapple (900g), chopped coarsely
1 small honeydew melon (1.3kg),
   chopped coarsely
1 small papaya (650g), chopped coarsely
2 small mangoes (600g), chopped coarsely
3 medium kiwifruits (255g), chopped coarsely
565g can lychees, drained, halved
¼ cup (60ml) lime juice
2 tablespoons passionfruit pulp
1 teaspoon finely grated whole nutmeg

1 Combine the water, sugar, ginger and star anise in small saucepan; stir over heat, without boiling, until sugar dissolves. Bring to the boil; reduce heat, simmer, uncovered, without stirring, about 10 minutes or until syrup thickens slightly. Cool.

2 Meanwhile, combine pineapple, melon, papaya, mango, kiwifruit and lychees in large bowl.

3 Combine juice, pulp and nutmeg in medium jug; stir in syrup. Pour syrup mixture over fruit. Cover; refrigerate 20 minutes before serving.

nutritional count per serving 0.9g total fat
(0g saturated fat); 920kJ (220 cal);
44.3g carbohydrate; 3.9g protein; 8.7g fibre

drinks order

hot mocha

preparation time 5 minutes
cooking time 5 minutes | serves 4

2 cups (500ml) milk
100g dark eating chocolate, chopped coarsely
2 cups (500ml) hot black coffee
1 teaspoon cocoa powder

1 Heat milk in medium saucepan, without boiling.
2 Meanwhile, divide chocolate among four
1¼-cup (310ml) glasses.
3 Stir coffee into milk then pour mixture into glasses.
Dust with sifted cocoa powder before serving.
nutritional count per 250ml *12.1g total fat*
(7.5g saturated fat); 920kJ (220 cal);
21.9g carbohydrate; 5.7g protein; 0.4g fibre

pineapple and rockmelon frappé

preparation time 10 minutes
makes 1.5 litres (6 cups)

1 small pineapple (900g), chopped coarsely
½ small rockmelon (650g), chopped coarsely
40 ice cubes, crushed
2 tablespoons finely chopped fresh mint

1 Blend or process pineapple and rockmelon,
in batches, until smooth; transfer to large jug.
2 Stir in ice and mint; pour into serving glasses.
Serve with fresh mint leaves, if you like.
nutritional count per 250ml *0.2g total fat*
(0g saturated fat); 213kJ (51 cal);
9.9g carbohydrate; 1.2g protein; 2.5g fibre

mixed berry smoothie

preparation time 5 minutes
makes 1.5 litres (6 cups)

2 cups (300g) frozen mixed berries
1¾ cups (480g) vanilla yogurt
2½ cups (625ml) milk
2 tablespoons honey

1 Blend or process ingredients until smooth.
Serve sprinkled with extra frozen mixed berries,
if you like.
nutritional count per 250ml *6.8g total fat*
(4.4g saturated fat); 711kJ (170 cal);
18.2g carbohydrate; 8.2g protein; 1.2g fibre

indian chai

preparation time 5 minutes
cooking time 10 minutes | makes 1 litre (4 cups)

5 cardamom pods, bruised
10 cloves
1 cinnamon stick
1cm piece fresh ginger (5g), sliced thickly
2 teaspoons fennel seeds
1 teaspoon vanilla extract
3 cups (750ml) water
4 darjeeling teabags
2 cups (500ml) milk
⅓ cup (90g) grated palm sugar

1 Combine cardamom, cloves, cinnamon, ginger,
fennel, extract and the water in medium saucepan;
bring to the boil. Cover; simmer 5 minutes. Remove
from heat; stand, covered, 10 minutes.
2 Return spice mixture to the boil, add teabags;
remove from heat. Stand 5 minutes.
3 Meanwhile, heat milk in medium saucepan
without boiling. Add milk to tea mixture; add sugar,
stir until dissolved.
nutritional count per 250ml *4.9g total fat*
(3.2g saturated fat); 727kJ (174 cal);
27.9g carbohydrate; 4.3g protein; 0g fibre

32

light meals and mains

preparation time 15 minutes | cooking time 40 minutes | serves 4

cheeseburgers with caramelised onion

500g beef mince
4 thin slices (40g) cheddar cheese
4 hamburger buns, split
1 small tomato (90g), sliced thinly
8 large butter lettuce leaves
4 large dill pickles (240g), sliced thinly
1 tablespoon american-style mustard
⅓ cup (95g) tomato sauce
caramelised onion
2 tablespoons olive oil
2 medium white onions (300g), sliced thinly
1 tablespoon brown sugar
2 tablespoons balsamic vinegar
2 tablespoons water

1 Make caramelised onion.

2 Shape beef into 4 patties; cook on heated oiled grill plate (or grill or barbecue) until cooked through. Top each patty with cheese slices during last minute of cooking time.

3 Meanwhile, toast buns, cut-sides down, on grill plate.

4 Place cheeseburgers, onion, tomato, lettuce and pickle between buns; serve with mustard and tomato sauce.

caramelised onion Heat oil in large frying pan; cook onion, stirring, until soft. Add sugar, vinegar and the water; cook, stirring, until onion is caramelised.

nutritional count per serving 23.6g total fat (7.4g saturated fat); 2378kJ (569 cal); 51.6g carbohydrate; 34.9g protein; 5g fibre

preparation time 15 minutes (plus refrigeration time) | cooking time 50 minutes | serves 4

steak sandwich with beetroot relish

While this recipe makes 2 cups of relish, you'll only need about half of it for these sandwiches. Keep the remaining relish in an airtight glass container in the refrigerator for up to 2 weeks.

¼ cup (60ml) light soy sauce
2 cloves garlic, crushed
400g beef rump steak
1 long french bread stick (300g)
175g watercress, trimmed
beetroot relish
1 tablespoon olive oil
10g butter
1 medium red onion (170g), sliced thinly
2 large beetroots (400g), peeled,
   grated coarsely
½ cup (125ml) red wine vinegar
1 cup (250ml) water
¾ cup (165g) caster sugar
1 cup (130g) dried cranberries
1½ tablespoons prepared horseradish

1 Combine sauce and garlic in medium bowl; add beef, turn to coat in mixture. Cover; refrigerate 1 hour.
2 Meanwhile, make beetroot relish.
3 Drain beef; cook on heated oiled grill plate (or grill or barbecue) until cooked as desired. Cover; stand 5 minutes then slice thinly.
4 Cut bread into quarters; slice each quarter in half horizontally. Divide beef among bread bases; top each with ¼ cup of the beetroot relish, a quarter of the watercress and remaining bread pieces.
beetroot relish Heat oil and butter in large deep saucepan; cook onion, stirring, until soft. Add beetroot; cook, stirring, 5 minutes. Add remaining ingredients; bring to the boil. Reduce heat; simmer, uncovered, about 35 minutes or until relish is thickened.
nutritional count per serving 13.2g total fat (4g saturated fat); 2730kJ (653 cal); 93.9g carbohydrate; 34.3g protein; 7.9g fibre

preparation time 10 minutes | cooking time 15 minutes | serves 4

spaghetti with pesto

2 cloves garlic, chopped coarsely
⅓ cup (50g) roasted pine nuts
½ cup (40g) finely grated parmesan cheese
2 cups firmly packed fresh basil leaves
½ cup (125ml) olive oil
500g spaghetti
½ cup (40g) flaked parmesan cheese

1 Blend or process garlic, nuts, grated cheese and basil until almost smooth. Gradually add oil in a thin, steady stream, processing until thick.
2 Cook pasta in large saucepan of boiling water, until just tender; drain, reserve ¼ cup of the cooking liquid.
3 Combine pasta, pesto and reserved cooking liquid in large bowl. Serve with flaked cheese.
nutritional count per serving *45.2g total fat (8.9g saturated fat); 3578kJ (859 cal); 86.2g carbohydrate; 23.6g protein; 5.6g fibre*

coppa and ricotta panini

We used coppa in this sandwich, but you can use parma ham or prosciutto, if you prefer. Coppa is a salted and dried sausage made from the neck or shoulder of pork. It is deep red in colour and can be found in both mild and spicy versions; it is more marbled with fat so it's less expensive.

⅓ cup (80g) black olive tapenade
¼ cup (60ml) balsamic vinegar
4 focaccia rolls (440g), halved
240g ricotta cheese
½ teaspoon finely grated lemon rind
1 teaspoon lemon juice
16 slices coppa (240g)
40g baby rocket leaves

1   Combine tapenade with 2 tablespoons of the vinegar in small bowl; spread over bottom half of each roll.
2   Combine cheese with rind and juice in small bowl; spread over tapenade.
3   Top ricotta with coppa and rocket; drizzle with remaining vinegar then top with roll halves.
4   Cook panini in preheated sandwich press until browned lightly and heated through.
nutritional count per serving 18.2g total fat *(6.7g saturated fat); 2036kJ (487 cal); 51.3g carbohydrate; 27.6g protein; 3g fibre*

turkish chicken club

You will need to buy two butter lettuces for this recipe.

⅓ cup (80ml) lime juice
2 tablespoons olive oil
2 teaspoons sumac
2 chicken thigh fillets (400g)
1 large turkish bread (430g)
1 lebanese cucumber (130g), sliced thinly
1 medium tomato (150g), sliced thinly
24 small butter lettuce leaves
coriander aïoli
½ cup (150g) mayonnaise
1 tablespoon lime juice
1 clove garlic, crushed
2 tablespoons finely chopped fresh coriander

1 Combine juice, oil, sumac and chicken in medium bowl, cover; refrigerate 30 minutes.

2 Meanwhile, make coriander aïoli.

3 Drain chicken; reserve marinade. Cook chicken on heated oiled grill plate (or grill or barbecue) until cooked through, brushing with reserved marinade after turning. Cover; stand 5 minutes then slice thinly.

4 Halve bread horizontally; cut each piece into 6 slices. Toast slices lightly.

5 Spread each toast slice with aïoli. Layer 4 toast slices with half the chicken, cucumber, tomato and lettuce, then top with toasts; layer with remaining chicken, cucumber, tomato and lettuce then top with remaining toast. Cut in half to serve, if you like.

coriander aïoli Combine ingredients in small bowl.

nutritional count per sandwich 32.1g total fat (5.4g saturated fat); 2700kJ (646 cal); 57.5g carbohydrate; 29.6g protein; 4.6g fibre

preparation time 10 minutes | cooking time 20 minutes | serves 4

corn and goat cheese quesadillas

A quesadilla (from queso, the Spanish word for cheese) is a tortilla "sandwich" containing cheese and any of a wide number of spicy filling ingredients, which is grilled, fried or toasted and usually served with salsa.

You need to buy two untrimmed corn cobs (800g) to get the amount of trimmed corn needed for this recipe.

2 corn cobs (500g) trimmed
240g soft goat cheese
8 large (20cm) flour tortillas
½ cup (100g) char-grilled capsicum, sliced thinly
40g jalapeño chilli slices, drained
⅓ cup coarsely chopped fresh coriander
20g butter
40g baby spinach leaves
1 lime, cut into wedges

1 Cook cobs on heated oiled grill plate (or grill or barbecue) until kernels are tender and browned lightly; when cool enough to handle, cut kernels from cobs.

2 Spread cheese gently over tortillas. Top 4 of the tortillas with corn, capsicum, chilli and coriander; top with remaining tortillas. Press around edges firmly to seal quesadillas.

3 Heat butter in medium frying pan; cook quesadillas, one at a time, until browned both sides and heated through.

4 Serve quesadillas with spinach and wedges.

nutritional count per serving *21.7g total fat (10g saturated fat); 2169kJ (519 cal); 57g carbohydrate; 19.8g protein; 8.6g fibre*

pizza for one

fetta and artichoke pizzetta

preparation time 5 minutes
cooking time 8 minutes

1 small (112g) pizza base
50g soft fetta cheese, crumbled
1 teaspoon olive oil
1 marinated artichoke (70g), sliced thinly
1 tablespoon fresh oregano leaves
2 teaspoons lime juice

1   Preheat oven to 220°C/200°C fan-forced.
Place pizza base on oven tray.
2   Combine 1 tablespoon of the cheese with oil.
Spread pizza base with cheese paste; top with
artichoke then sprinkle with remaining cheese.
3   Bake about 8 minutes.
4   Serve pizzetta sprinkled with oregano and juice.
nutritional count per serving *22g total fat
(9.2g saturated fat); 2223kJ (532 cal);
60.8g carbohydrate; 20.3g protein; 4.2g fibre*

moroccan pizzetta

preparation time 5 minutes
cooking time 8 minutes

You need to buy half a small barbecued
chicken for this recipe.

1 small (112g) pizza base
2 tablespoons hummus
½ cup (80g) shredded barbecued chicken
30g preserved lemon, rinsed, sliced thinly
30g haloumi cheese, sliced thinly
1 tablespoon fresh flat-leaf parsley leaves
1 teaspoon olive oil

1   Preheat oven to 220°C/200°C fan-forced.
Place pizza base on oven tray.
2   Spread pizza base with hummus; top with
chicken, lemon then cheese.
3   Bake about 8 minutes.
4   Serve pizzetta sprinkled with parsley and oil.
nutritional count per serving *22.7g total fat
(7g saturated fat); 2679kJ (641 cal);
64.3g carbohydrate; 40.2g protein; 8.6g fibre*

We used small (15cm diameter) packaged pizza bases for all four of these recipes.

pepperoni pizzetta

preparation time 5 minutes
cooking time 8 minutes

1 small (112g) pizza base
2 tablespoons tomato paste
40g pepperoni, sliced thinly
1 fresh small red thai chilli, sliced thinly
¼ cup (20g) flaked parmesan cheese
15g wild rocket leaves
2 teaspoons lemon juice

1 Preheat oven to 220°C/200°C fan-forced. Place pizza base on oven tray.
2 Spread pizza base with paste; top with pepperoni then sprinkle with chilli.
3 Bake about 8 minutes.
4 Combine cheese, rocket and juice in small bowl. Serve pizzetta topped with rocket salad.
nutritional count per serving *25.4g total fat (9.9g saturated fat); 2592kJ (620 cal); 65.5g carbohydrate; 29g protein; 6.2g fibre*

pizzetta caprese

preparation time 5 minutes
cooking time 8 minutes

1 small (112g) pizza base
2 cherry bocconcini cheeses (30g), sliced thinly
½ clove garlic, sliced thinly
1 small tomato (90g), sliced thinly
1 tablespoon fresh basil leaves

1 Preheat oven to 220°C/200°C fan-forced. Place pizza base on oven tray.
2 Place cheese and garlic on pizza base.
3 Bake about 8 minutes.
4 Serve pizzetta topped with tomato and basil.
nutritional count per serving *9g total fat (3.6g saturated fat); 1693kJ (405 cal); 61.3g carbohydrate; 16.3g protein; 5.6g fibre*

caesar salad with salt and pepper squid

1 tablespoon sichuan peppercorns
2 tablespoons sea salt
1 cup (200g) rice flour
600g cleaned squid hoods with tentacles
vegetable oil, for deep-frying
1 tablespoon sea salt, extra
2 baby cos lettuces (360g)
caesar dressing
1 cup (300g) mayonnaise
1 clove garlic, crushed
2 tablespoons lime juice
1 tablespoon milk
1 teaspoon worcestershire sauce

1 Dry-fry peppercorns in small frying pan until fragrant; using mortar and pestle, crush peppercorns coarsely. Combine crushed pepper, salt and flour in medium bowl.

2 Cut squid hoods down centre to open out; score inside in diagonal pattern then cut into thick strips. Toss squid pieces in flour mixture; shake off excess.

3 Make caesar dressing.

4 Heat oil in wok; deep-fry squid, in batches, until browned lightly. Drain on absorbent paper; sprinkle with extra salt.

5 Divide leaves among serving plates; top with squid, drizzle with dressing.

caesar dressing Whisk ingredients in small bowl.

nutritional count per serving *34.7g total fat (4.5g saturated fat); 2688kJ (643 cal); 51g carbohydrate; 30g protein; 3.7g fibre*

crab cakes with avocado salsa

Crab meat is available from fishmongers or supermarkets. If frozen, thaw then drain well before use.

600g cooked crab meat
1 cup (70g) stale white breadcrumbs
1 egg
1 clove garlic, crushed
2 tablespoons mayonnaise
¼ cup finely chopped fresh coriander
½ teaspoon cayenne pepper
15g butter
1 tablespoon olive oil

avocado salsa
2 small avocados (400g), chopped coarsely
1 medium tomato (150g), chopped coarsely
¾ cup loosely packed fresh coriander leaves
2 teaspoons Tabasco
1 tablespoon lime juice
1 tablespoon olive oil

1 Combine crab meat, breadcrumbs, egg, garlic, mayonnaise, coriander and pepper in medium bowl. Shape mixture into eight patties; place on tray. Cover; refrigerate 1 hour.
2 Meanwhile, make avocado salsa.
3 Heat butter and oil in large frying pan; cook crab cakes, in batches, until browned both sides and heated through. Serve crab cakes topped with salsa.
avocado salsa Combine ingredients in medium bowl.

nutritional count per serving *34.1g total fat (7.8g saturated fat); 2011kJ (481 cal); 17.6g carbohydrate; 25.3g protein; 2.8g fibre*

greek salad with grilled lamb

¼ cup (70g) yogurt
⅓ cup (80ml) lemon juice
¼ cup (60ml) olive oil
2 cloves garlic, crushed
600g lamb fillets
3 medium tomatoes (450g), cut
    into thin wedges
1 small red onion (100g), sliced thinly
2 medium red capsicums (400g),
    chopped coarsely
2 lebanese cucumbers (260g),
    chopped coarsely
½ cup (75g) seeded kalamata olives
400g can chickpeas, rinsed, drained
1 cup firmly packed fresh
    flat-leaf parsley leaves
100g fetta cheese, crumbled

1 Combine yogurt, 1 tablespoon of the juice, 1 tablespoon of the oil and half the garlic in medium bowl, add lamb; mix well. Cover; refrigerate until needed.
2 Meanwhile, combine remaining juice, oil and garlic in screw-top jar; shake well.
3 Drain lamb; cook on heated oiled grill plate (or grill or barbecue) until cooked as desired. Cover; stand 5 minutes then slice thickly.
4 Combine remaining ingredients in large bowl with lemon dressing. Serve salad topped with lamb.

nutritional count per serving 27.5g total fat (8.8g saturated fat); 2215kJ (530 cal); 23.1g carbohydrate; 44g protein; 7.8g fibre

50

pear and roquefort salad

1 small french bread stick (150g), sliced thinly
100g roquefort cheese, softened
2 small pears (360g), sliced thinly
1 cup (110g) coarsely chopped roasted walnuts
1 butter lettuce, leaves separated
100g baby spinach leaves
buttermilk dressing
¼ cup (60ml) buttermilk
1 tablespoon lemon juice
1 tablespoon olive oil
½ teaspoon caster sugar
1 clove garlic, crushed

1   Preheat oven to 200°C/180°C fan-forced.
2   Place bread on oven tray; toast, in oven, until browned both sides.
3   Meanwhile, make buttermilk dressing.
4   Spread toast with cheese.
5   Place remaining ingredients in large serving bowl; add dressing, toss gently to combine. Serve salad with cheese toast.
buttermilk dressing Whisk ingredients in medium bowl.
nutritional count per serving *33.7g total fat (7.4g saturated fat); 2082kJ (498 cal); 31.2g carbohydrate; 14.6g protein; 7.7g fibre*

couscous salad with haloumi

1½ cups (300g) couscous
1½ cups (375ml) boiling water
¼ cup (60ml) lemon juice
¼ cup (60ml) olive oil
1 teaspoon ground cumin
½ cup (70g) coarsely chopped dried dates
½ cup (70g) roasted slivered almonds
¾ cup coarsely chopped fresh mint
2 x 250g packets haloumi cheese,
    sliced thickly

1 Combine couscous with the water in large
heatproof bowl, cover; stand about 5 minutes or
until liquid is absorbed, fluffing with fork occasionally.
2 Combine juice, oil and cumin in screw-top jar;
shake well.
3 Add cumin dressing, dates, nuts and mint to
couscous; mix gently.
4 Heat oiled large frying pan; cook cheese
until browned both sides. Serve salad topped
with cheese.
nutritional count per serving *45.4g total fat
(16.4g saturated fat); 3641kJ (871 cal);
73g carbohydrate; 46.6g protein; 4.6g fibre*

preparation time 25 minutes (plus refrigeration time) | cooking time 1 hour | makes 12

lamb korma pies

20g butter
2 tablespoons olive oil
600g lamb fillets, chopped coarsely
1 medium brown onion (150g), sliced thinly
1 clove garlic, crushed
2cm piece fresh ginger (10g), grated
¼ cup (20g) roasted flaked almonds
⅓ cup (100g) korma paste
⅓ cup (80ml) chicken stock
½ cup (140g) yogurt
1 cup (120g) frozen peas
1 tablespoon lemon juice
⅓ cup firmly packed fresh coriander leaves
6 sheets ready-rolled puff pastry
1 egg, beaten lightly

1   Heat half the butter with half the oil in large saucepan; cook lamb, in batches, until browned.
2   Heat remaining butter and oil in same pan; cook onion, garlic and ginger, stirring, until onion softens. Add nuts and paste; cook, stirring, until fragrant.
3   Return lamb to pan with stock and yogurt; simmer, uncovered, about 20 minutes or until sauce thickens. Stir in peas, juice and coriander. Cool.

4   Lightly oil two 6-hole (¾-cup/180ml) texas muffin pans. Cut two 13cm rounds from opposite corners of each pastry sheet; cut two 9cm rounds from remaining corners of each sheet. Place the 12 large rounds in pan holes to cover bases and sides. Prick bases with fork; refrigerate 30 minutes. Cover small rounds with damp cloth; refrigerate.
5   Preheat oven to 200°C/180°C fan-forced.
6   Cover pastry-lined pan holes with baking paper; fill with dried beans or uncooked rice. Bake, 10 minutes. Remove paper and beans carefully from pan holes; cool pastry cases.
7   Fill pastry cases with lamb mixture. Brush pastry edges with egg; top pies with small pastry rounds, pressing edges to seal.
8   Brush pies with remaining egg; bake about 15 minutes. Stand 5 minutes before serving. Serve with mango chutney and raita, if you like.
nutritional count per pie *29.6g total fat (13.1g saturated fat); 1977kJ (473 cal); 32.9g carbohydrate; 17.7g protein; 3g fibre*

black-eyed bean and ham soup

You need to buy half a bunch of untrimmed silver beet (500g) for this recipe.

1 cup (200g) black-eyed beans
1 tablespoon olive oil
1 trimmed celery stalk (100g), chopped coarsely
1 small brown onion (80g), chopped coarsely
1 medium carrot (120g), chopped coarsely
1 bay leaf
2 cloves garlic
1.2kg ham hock
1 litre (4 cups) chicken stock
2 litres (8 cups) water
½ bunch trimmed silver beet (125g), shredded finely
2 tablespoons cider vinegar

1   Place beans in medium bowl, cover with water; stand overnight, rinse, drain.
2   Heat oil in large saucepan, add celery, onion and carrot; cook until vegetables are soft. Add bay leaf, garlic, ham hock, stock and the water; bring to the boil. Reduce heat; simmer, uncovered, 1 hour.
3   Add beans to soup; simmer, uncovered, about 1 hour or until beans are tender.
4   Remove hock from soup. When cool enough to handle, remove meat from hock. Discard bone; shred meat coarsely, return to soup.
5   Add silver beet to soup; cook, stirring, until wilted. Remove from heat; stir in vinegar.
nutritional count per serving *7.2g total fat (1.8g saturated fat); 945kJ (226 cal); 16.1g carbohydrate; 21.2g protein; 6.3g fibre*

delicious dips

moroccan carrot dip

preparation time 10 minutes
cooking time 20 minutes | makes 2 cups

4 medium carrots (480g), chopped coarsely
2 cloves garlic, peeled
1 teaspoon ground cumin
1 tablespoon honey
2 tablespoons lemon juice
¼ cup (70g) greek-style yogurt
1 tablespoon coarsely chopped fresh
   coriander leaves

1 Cover carrots and garlic with water in small saucepan; bring to the boil. Reduce heat; simmer, covered, about 20 minutes or until carrots are soft. Drain.
2 Blend or process carrot mixture with cumin, honey and juice until smooth. Add yogurt; blend until smooth.
3 Sprinkle dip with coriander.
nutritional count per tablespoon *0.2g total fat (0.1g saturated fat); 46kJ (11 cal); 1.9g carbohydrate; 0.3g protein; 0.5g fibre*

artichoke spinach dip

preparation time 10 minutes
cooking time 20 minutes | makes 2 cups

340g jar marinated artichokes, rinsed, drained
250g frozen chopped spinach, thawed
½ cup (120g) sour cream
¼ cup (75g) mayonnaise
¾ cup (60g) coarsely grated parmesan cheese
1 clove garlic, crushed

1 Preheat oven to 200°C/180°C fan-forced.
2 Chop artichokes coarsely; combine with remaining ingredients in medium bowl.
3 Transfer dip mixture to 2-cup (500ml) ovenproof dish; cook, covered, 20 minutes.
nutritional count per tablespoon *2.7g total fat (1.3g saturated fat); 130kJ (31 cal); 0.7g carbohydrate; 1.1g protein; 0.4g fibre*

Serve each of these dips with a warmed large loaf of turkish bread (about 430g), cut into fingers.

black olive tapenade

preparation time 5 minutes | makes 1 cup

2 cups (240g) seeded black olives
1 anchovy fillet, rinsed, drained
1 tablespoon capers, rinsed, drained
2 teaspoons dijon mustard
2 tablespoons olive oil

1   Rinse and drain olives on absorbent paper. Blend or process olives with anchovy, capers and mustard until smooth.
2   With motor operating, add oil in a thin steady stream, processing until tapenade is smooth.
nutritional count per tablespoon *3.3g total fat (0.5g saturated fat); 213kJ (51 cal); 4.6g carbohydrate; 0.6g protein; 0.3g fibre*

white bean dip

preparation time 5 minutes | makes 2 cups

Many varieties of cooked white beans are available canned, among them cannelloni (which is what we used), butter and haricot beans; any of these is suitable for this dip.

2 x 400g cans white beans, rinsed, drained
2 cloves garlic, crushed
2 tablespoons lemon juice
⅓ cup (80ml) olive oil
1 tablespoon fresh basil leaves

1   Blend or process beans, garlic, juice and oil until almost smooth.
2   Sprinkle dip with basil.
nutritional count per tablespoon *3.1g total fat (0.4g saturated fat); 138kJ (33 cal); 0.6g carbohydrate; 0.5g protein; 0.9g fibre*

seafood chowder

1 tablespoon olive oil
3 rindless bacon rashers (195g), sliced thinly
1 medium brown onion (150g), chopped finely
1 small fennel bulb (200g), sliced thinly
3 cloves garlic, sliced thinly
2 medium tomatoes (300g), seeded,
    chopped coarsely
2 tablespoons tomato paste
1 teaspoon hot paprika
½ cup (125ml) dry white wine
2 x 400g cans whole tomatoes
3 cups (750ml) fish stock
1 litre (4 cups) water
500g kipfler potatoes, cut into 3cm pieces
1.2kg marinara mix
½ cup coarsely chopped fresh flat-leaf parsley

1   Heat oil in large saucepan, add bacon; cook until crisp. Drain on absorbent paper.
2   Add onion, fennel and garlic to pan; cook until vegetables soften. Add fresh tomato; cook until soft. Add tomato paste and paprika; cook, stirring, 2 minutes. Return bacon to pan with wine; cook, stirring, 2 minutes.
3   Slice canned tomatoes thickly. Add slices with juice from can, stock, the water and potato to pan; bring to the boil. Reduce heat; simmer, covered, about 20 minutes or until potato is soft.
4   Add marinara mix; cook, covered, about 3 minutes. Stir in parsley.

nutritional count per serving *8.8g total fat (2.2g saturated fat); 1781kJ (426 cal); 24.5g carbohydrate; 50.5g protein; 5.7g fibre*

preparation time 25 minutes | cooking time 30 minutes | serves 4

classic fish and chips

Reheat the oil between frying batches of chips and fish.

1 cup (150g) self-raising flour
1 cup (250ml) dry ale
1 tablespoon sea salt
1kg potatoes, peeled
peanut oil, for deep-frying
4 x 150g blue-eye fillets, halved lengthways
tartar sauce
⅔ cup (200g) whole-egg mayonnaise
½ small brown onion (40g), chopped finely
2 tablespoons finely chopped cornichons
1 tablespoon capers, rinsed, drained,
   chopped finely
1 tablespoon finely chopped
   fresh flat-leaf parsley
1 tablespoon lemon juice

1 Make tartar sauce.
2 Sift flour into medium bowl; whisk in beer and salt until smooth.
3 Cut potatoes lengthways into 1cm slices; cut each slice lengthways into 1cm-chips; dry with absorbent paper.
4 Heat oil in large saucepan. Cook chips, in three batches, about 2 minutes or until tender but not brown. Drain on absorbent paper.
5 Dip fish in batter; drain away excess. Deep-fry fish, in batches, until cooked. Drain on absorbent paper.
6 Deep-fry chips, in three batches, until crisp and golden brown; drain on absorbent paper. Serve fish and chips with sauce and lemon wedges, if you like.
tartar sauce Combine ingredients in medium bowl.
nutritional count per serving *38.3g total fat (6.2g saturated fat); 3340kJ (799 cal); 66.1g carbohydrate; 40.3g protein; 5.4g fibre*

gazpacho

1kg ripe tomatoes, peeled, chopped coarsely
2 lebanese cucumbers (260g), seeded,
   chopped coarsely
2 large red capsicums (700g), chopped coarsely
1 large green capsicum (350g), chopped coarsely
1 large red onion (200g), chopped coarsely
2 cloves garlic, chopped coarsely
415ml can tomato juice
2 tablespoons red wine vinegar
1 tablespoon olive oil
2 teaspoons Tabasco
1 medium avocado (250g), chopped finely
1 small yellow capsicum (150g), chopped finely
¼ cup finely chopped fresh coriander

1 Blend or process tomatoes, cucumber,
capsicums, onion, garlic, juice, vinegar,
oil and Tabasco, in batches, until smooth.
Pour into large jug. Cover; refrigerate 3 hours.
2 Stir soup; pour into serving bowls, top
with remaining ingredients. Serve gazpacho
sprinkled with extra Tabasco, if you like.
nutritional count per serving *10.4g total fat
(1.9g saturated fat); 786kJ (188 cal);
14.5g carbohydrate; 6.2g protein; 6.3g fibre*

lentil and garlic soup with yogurt

1 tablespoon olive oil
10 cloves garlic, sliced thinly
2 sprigs fresh thyme
2 cups (400g) australian fine green lentils
2 cups (500ml) vegetable stock
2 litres (8 cups) water
175g watercress, trimmed, chopped coarsely
minted yogurt
1 cup (280g) yogurt
1 tablespoon lemon juice
¼ cup coarsely chopped fresh mint

1   Heat oil in large saucepan; cook garlic and thyme, stirring, until garlic softens. Stir in lentils then stock and the water; bring to the boil. Reduce heat; simmer, covered, about 35 minutes or until lentils soften.
2   Meanwhile, make minted yogurt.
3   Blend or process soup, in batches, until pureed; return to pan. Add watercress to soup; cook, stirring, until wilted. Serve soup with minted yogurt.
minted yogurt Combine ingredients in medium bowl.

nutritional count per serving *6.5g total fat (1.9g saturated fat); 1158kJ (277 cal); 28.9g carbohydrate; 20.1g protein; 16.7g fibre*

64

herbed chicken schnitzel

4 chicken breast fillets (800g)
¼ cup (35g) plain flour
2 eggs
1 tablespoon milk
2½ cups (175g) stale white breadcrumbs
2 teaspoons finely grated lemon rind
2 tablespoons finely chopped
    fresh flat-leaf parsley
2 tablespoons finely chopped fresh basil
⅓ cup (25g) finely grated parmesan cheese
vegetable oil, for shallow-frying
green bean salad
250g baby green beans, trimmed
2 tablespoons lemon juice
1 tablespoon olive oil
⅓ cup coarsely chopped fresh flat-leaf parsley

1 Using meat mallet, gently pound chicken, one piece at a time, between sheets of plastic wrap until 5mm thick; cut each piece in half.
2 Whisk flour, eggs and milk in shallow bowl; combine breadcrumbs, rind, herbs and cheese in another shallow bowl. Coat chicken pieces, one at a time, in egg mixture then breadcrumb mixture.
3 Heat oil in large frying pan; shallow-fry chicken, in batches, until cooked. Drain on absorbent paper.
4 Meanwhile, make green bean salad; serve salad with chicken, and lemon wedges, if you like.
green bean salad Boil, steam or microwave beans until tender; drain. Toss beans in medium bowl with remaining ingredients.
nutritional count per serving *28.1g total fat (5.9g saturated fat); 2746kJ (657 cal); 38.5g carbohydrate; 59.9g protein; 4.6g fibre*

preparation time 1 hour | cooking time 1 hour 40 minutes | serves 8

italian sausage and three-cheese lasagne

500g italian sausages
250g frozen chopped spinach, thawed, drained
250g ricotta cheese
¼ teaspoon ground nutmeg
½ cup (40g) finely grated parmesan cheese
1 egg
6 sheets fresh lasagne
250g mozzarella cheese, sliced thinly

tomato sauce

1 tablespoon olive oil
1 medium onion (150g), chopped finely
1 medium carrot (120g), chopped finely
1 trimmed celery stalk (100g), chopped finely
5 x 8cm long parsley stalks, crushed
2 cloves garlic, crushed
½ cup (125ml) dry red wine
¼ cup (70g) tomato paste
700g bottled tomato pasta sauce

cheese sauce

50g butter
⅓ cup (50g) plain flour
2 cups (500ml) milk
1½ cups (120g) finely grated parmesan cheese

1 Make tomato sauce. Make cheese sauce.
2 Preheat oven to 200°C/180°C fan-forced.
3 Cook sausages in oiled large frying pan until browned all over; drain then slice thinly.
4 Combine spinach, ricotta, nutmeg, parmesan and egg in medium bowl.

5 Spread ½ cup of the cheese sauce over base of 20cm x 30cm ovenproof dish. Top with two pasta sheets then spread with half the spinach mixture. Sprinkle with half the sausage; cover with 1 cup of the tomato sauce then half the remaining cheese sauce.
6 Top with two pasta sheets. Spread remaining spinach mixture over pasta; sprinkle with remaining sausage. Spread with 1 cup tomato sauce, then remaining cheese sauce.
7 Top with remaining pasta, then half the remaining tomato sauce. Top with mozzarella; spread with remaining tomato sauce.
8 Bake lasagne, covered, 30 minutes. Uncover, bake about 10 minutes or until browned lightly. Stand 10 minutes before serving.

tomato sauce Heat oil in large saucepan, add onion, carrot, celery and parsley; cook, stirring occasionally, until vegetables soften. Add garlic; cook, stirring, 1 minute. Add wine; cook, stirring, until almost evaporated. Discard parsley stalks. Add paste; cook, stirring, 3 minutes. Add sauce; simmer, uncovered, about 15 minutes.

cheese sauce Melt butter in medium saucepan, add flour; cook, stirring, until mixture thickens and bubbles. Gradually add milk; stir until mixture boils and thickens. Reduce heat; cook, stirring, 1 minute, remove from heat. Add cheese, stir until melted.

nutritional count per serving *46.8g total fat (23.1g saturated fat); 3227kJ (772 cal); 44g carbohydrate; 39.3g protein; 5.4g fibre*

mushroom risotto

3 cups (750ml) chicken stock
1 litre (4 cups) water
2 tablespoons olive oil
1 small brown onion (80g), chopped finely
10g butter
2 cloves garlic, sliced thinly
100g shiitake mushrooms, sliced thinly
100g button mushrooms, sliced thinly
100g oyster mushrooms, sliced thinly
2 cups (400g) arborio rice
½ cup (125ml) dry white wine
75g baby spinach leaves
⅓ cup (25g) coarsely grated parmesan cheese
⅓ cup (50g) roasted pine nuts
¼ cup finely chopped fresh chives

1 Place stock and the water in large saucepan; bring to the boil. Reduce heat; simmer, covered.

2 Heat oil in large saucepan; cook onion, stirring, until soft. Add butter, garlic and mushrooms; cook, stirring, until vegetables soften. Add rice; stir to coat in mixture. Add wine; cook, stirring until liquid is almost evaporated.

3 Stir 1 cup simmering stock mixture into rice mixture; cook, stirring, over low heat until liquid is absorbed. Continue adding stock mixture in 1-cup batches, stirring, until absorbed after each addition. Total cooking time should be about 35 minutes or until rice is tender.

4 Stir spinach and cheese into risotto. Remove from heat; stir in nuts and half the chives. Serve sprinkled with remaining chives.

nutritional count per serving *15.7g total fat (3.3g saturated fat); 1781kJ (426 cal); 55.2g carbohydrate; 16.8g protein; 3.3g fibre*

quick snacks

bruschetta

preparation time 10 minutes (plus standing time)
cooking time 5 minutes | makes 12

2 medium tomatoes (300g), seeded,
   chopped finely
½ small red onion (50g), chopped finely
1 clove garlic, crushed
1 tablespoon red wine vinegar
2 tablespoons olive oil
1 small french bread stick (150g),
   sliced into 2.5cm slices
cooking-oil spray
2 tablespoons finely shredded fresh basil

1   Preheat oven to 220°C/200°C fan-forced.
2   Combine tomato, onion, garlic, vinegar and
oil in small bowl. Stand 20 minutes.
3   Meanwhile, place bread on oiled oven tray;
spray with cooking oil. Toast, in oven (or under
grill), until browned both sides.
4   Stir basil into tomato mixture, spoon over toast.
nutritional count per bruschetta *4.3g total fat*
(0.5g saturated fat); 318kJ (76 cal);
7.4g carbohydrate; 1.5g protein; 0.9g fibre

bean nachos

preparation time 10 minutes
cooking time 10 minutes | serves 6

2 x 420g cans kidney beans, rinsed, drained
⅓ cup (85g) chunky tomato salsa
⅓ cup finely chopped fresh coriander
230g bag corn chips
1½ cups (180g) coarsely grated cheddar cheese
2 cups (120g) finely shredded iceberg lettuce
1 small tomato (90g), chopped coarsely
½ small avocado (100g), chopped coarsely
2 tablespoons lime juice

1   Preheat oven to 220°C/200°C fan-forced.
2   Combine half the beans with salsa; mash until
chunky. Stir in remaining beans and coriander.
3   Spread half the chips in medium shallow baking
dish; top with half the cheese and half the bean
mixture. Top with remaining chips, remaining cheese
then remaining bean mixture. Cook 10 minutes.
4   Toss lettuce, tomato and avocado in medium
bowl with juice. Serve nachos topped with salad.
nutritional count per serving *24.5g total fat*
(11.6g saturated fat); 1856kJ (444 cal);
33.7g carbohydrate; 17.3g protein; 10.8g fibre

thai chicken skewers

preparation time 10 minutes
(plus refrigeration time)
cooking time 5 minutes | makes 12

2 chicken thigh fillets (400g)
2 tablespoons light soy sauce
2 tablespoons grated palm sugar
¼ cup (60ml) lime juice

satay sauce
¼ cup (70g) crunchy peanut butter
1 tablespoon light soy sauce
2 teaspoons brown sugar
1 tablespoon lime juice
¼ cup (60ml) light coconut milk

1   Cut each fillet into 6 long slices; thread onto skewers. Combine remaining ingredients in small shallow baking dish; add skewers, turn to coat in marinade. Cover; refrigerate 1 hour.
2   Meanwhile, make satay sauce.
3   Cook drained skewers on heated oiled grill plate. Serve drizzled with sauce.
satay sauce   Stir ingredients in small saucepan until heated.
nutritional count per skewer *6g total fat (1.8g saturated fat); 426kJ (102 cal); 3.7g carbohydrate; 8.2g protein; 0.6g fibre*

vietnamese prawn rolls

preparation time 20 minutes | makes 12

50g rice vermicelli, soaked, drained
¼ small wombok (175g), shredded finely
½ cup loosely packed fresh mint leaves, torn
2 teaspoons brown sugar
2 tablespoons lime juice
500g cooked medium king prawns
12 x 21cm rice paper rounds

hoisin dipping sauce
½ cup (125ml) hoisin sauce
2 tablespoons rice vinegar

1   Combine chopped vermicelli in medium bowl with wombok, mint, sugar and juice.
2   Shell and devein prawns; chop meat finely.
3   Meanwhile, make hoisin dipping sauce.
4   Dip 1 rice paper round into bowl of warm water until soft; place on board covered with tea towel. Top with a little of the prawn meat and noodle filling. Fold and roll to enclose filling. Repeat with remaining rounds, prawn meat and noodle filling.
5   Serve with hoisin dipping sauce.
hoisin dipping sauce   Combine ingredients in bowl.
nutritional count per roll *0.9g total fat (0.1g saturated fat); 326kJ (78 cal); 10.8g carbohydrate; 5.5g protein; 1.7g fibre*

preparation time 25 minutes | cooking time 45 minutes | serves 6

gruyère, leek and bacon tart

50g butter

2 medium leeks (700g), sliced thinly

2 rindless bacon rashers (130g), chopped finely

2 sheets ready-rolled puff pastry

2 eggs

½ cup (125ml) cream

1 teaspoon fresh thyme leaves

½ cup (60g) finely grated gruyère cheese

1 Preheat oven to 220°C/200°C fan-forced. Oil 24cm-round loose-based flan tin; place tin on oven tray.

2 Melt butter in medium frying pan; cook leek, stirring occasionally, about 15 minutes or until soft. Remove from pan. Cook bacon in same pan, stirring, until crisp; drain on absorbent paper.

3 Meanwhile, place one pastry sheet in flan tin; overlap with second sheet to form cross shape, trim away overlapping pastry. Prick pastry base with fork, cover with baking paper; fill with dried beans or uncooked rice. Bake 20 minutes. Remove paper and beans; cool pastry case. Reduce oven to 200°C/180°C fan-forced.

4 Whisk eggs, cream and thyme in small bowl.

5 Spread leek into pastry case; top with bacon. Pour in egg mixture; sprinkle with cheese. Bake, about 20 minutes or until filling sets. Cool 10 minutes before serving. Serve with a baby rocket and parmesan salad, if you like.

nutritional count per serving *34.8g total fat (20.2g saturated fat); 1948kJ (466 cal); 24.5g carbohydrate; 14.4g protein; 2.8g fibre*

preparation time 20 minutes | cooking time 25 minutes | serves 4

potato frittata with smoked salmon

You will need a medium ovenproof frying pan with a 17cm base for this recipe.

20g butter
1 tablespoon olive oil
2 medium potatoes (400g), cut into 1cm pieces
1 green onion, chopped finely
8 eggs
¼ cup (60ml) cream
⅓ cup (25g) finely grated parmesan cheese
1 tablespoon finely chopped fresh dill
200g smoked salmon
2 tablespoons sour cream

1 Preheat oven to 220°C/200°C fan-forced.
2 Heat butter and oil in medium frying pan; cook potato, stirring occasionally, until browned and tender. Add onion; cook, stirring gently, 1 minute.
3 Meanwhile, whisk eggs, cream, cheese and dill in medium jug. Pour into pan; stir gently. Cook frittata over medium heat, about 2 minutes or until bottom sets. Place pan in oven; cook, uncovered, about 10 minutes or until frittata sets.
4 Slide frittata onto serving plate; serve topped with salmon, sour cream and some extra dill, if you like.

nutritional count per serving *34.1g total fat (15.2g saturated fat); 2031kJ (486 cal); 14.3g carbohydrate; 30.2g protein; 2.1g fibre*

sweets

preparation time 10 minutes | cooking time 1 hour 10 minutes | makes 12 slices

banana bread

You need two large overripe bananas (460g) for this recipe.

90g unsalted butter, softened
1 teaspoon vanilla extract
1 cup (220g) firmly packed brown sugar
2 eggs
1 cup mashed banana
1 cup (150g) plain flour
1 cup (150g) self-raising flour

1 Preheat oven to 180°C/160°C fan-forced. Grease 14cm x 21cm loaf pan; line base and long sides with baking paper, extending paper 5cm above long sides.
2 Beat butter, extract and sugar in small bowl with electric mixer until light and fluffy. Beat in eggs, one at a time. Transfer mixture to large bowl; stir in banana then sifted flours, in two batches.
3 Spread mixture into pan; cover with a strip of pleated foil. Bake 40 minutes; uncover, bake about 30 minutes. Stand 5 minutes; lift onto wire rack to cool. Serve toasted or warm, with butter if you like.
nutritional count per slice *9.5g total fat (5.6g saturated fat); 1296kJ (309 cal); 49.7g carbohydrate; 5.1g protein; 1.7g fibre*

preparation time 20 minutes | cooking time 20 minutes | makes 15

buttermilk scones with strawberries & cream

3 cups (450g) self-raising flour
2 tablespoons caster sugar
40g unsalted butter
2 cups (500ml) buttermilk
2 tablespoons buttermilk, extra
300ml thickened cream
250g strawberries, halved

1 Preheat oven to 240°C/220°C fan-forced.
Grease 20cm x 30cm lamington pan.
2 Sift flour and sugar into large bowl; rub in butter
with fingertips.
3 Add buttermilk; use knife to "cut" buttermilk
through the mixture to form a soft, sticky dough.
Knead dough lightly on floured surface until smooth.
4 Press dough out to an even 2.5cm thickness.
Dip 6.5cm cutter into flour; cut as many rounds as
possible from the dough. Place scones side by
side, just touching, in pan.
5 Gently knead scraps of dough together; repeat
pressing and cutting of dough, place in pan. Brush
tops with extra buttermilk; bake about 20 minutes
or until scones sound hollow when tapped firmly
on the top.
6 Meanwhile, beat cream in small bowl with electric
mixer until soft peaks form. Serve scones with
whipped cream and strawberries.
nutritional count per scone *9.9g total fat
(6.3g saturated fat); 869kJ (208 cal);
24.4g carbohydrate; 4.8g protein; 1.4g fibre*

preparation time 10 minutes | cooking time 20 minutes | makes 6

berry yogurt muffins

We used a mixture of raspberries and blueberries in these muffins.

1½ cups (225g) self-raising flour
⅓ cup (30g) rolled oats
3 eggs
¾ cup (165g) firmly packed brown sugar
¾ cup (200g) yogurt
⅓ cup (80ml) vegetable oil
180g fresh or frozen berries

1 Preheat oven to 200°C/180°C fan-forced. Grease six-hole (¾-cup/180ml) texas muffin pan.
2 Combine sifted flour with oats in medium bowl. Stir in eggs, sugar, yogurt and oil; add berries, stir gently into muffin mixture.
3 Spoon mixture into pan holes; bake about 20 minutes. Stand 5 minutes before turning, top-side up, onto wire rack to cool.
nutritional count per muffin *16.9g total fat (3.2g saturated fat); 1806kJ (432 cal); 58.8g carbohydrate; 9.7g protein; 2.5g fibre*

preparation time 25 minutes | cooking time 30 minutes | makes 12

portuguese custard tarts

½ cup (110g) caster sugar
2 tablespoons cornflour
4 egg yolks
300ml cream
⅓ cup (80ml) water
3cm strip lemon rind
1 teaspoon vanilla extract
1 sheet ready-rolled sweet puff pastry

1 Preheat oven to 220°C/200°C fan-forced.
Grease 12-hole (⅓-cup/80ml) muffin pan.
2 Combine sugar and cornflour in medium
saucepan; whisk in egg yolks, cream and the
water. Add rind; stir over medium heat until
mixture comes to the boil. Remove from heat;
discard rind. Stir extract into custard.
3 Cut pastry sheet in half; place halves on top of
each other. Roll pastry tightly (like a swiss roll) from
one short side; cut roll into twelve 1cm rounds.
4 Place pastry rounds, cut-sides up, on lightly
floured surface; roll each into a 10cm round. Push
rounds into pan holes; spoon in custard.
5 Bake tarts about 20 minutes. Stand 5 minutes,
before lifting onto wire rack to cool.
nutritional count per tart *14.3g total fat*
(8.3g saturated fat); 849kJ (203 cal);
16.5g carbohydrate; 2.4g protein; 0.2g fibre

dark chocolate mud cake

250g unsalted butter, chopped
2 cups (440g) caster sugar
½ cup (125ml) milk
½ cup (125ml) strong black coffee
½ cup (125ml) bourbon
1 teaspoon vanilla extract
200g dark eating chocolate, chopped coarsely
1½ cups (225g) plain flour
¼ cup (35g) self-raising flour
¼ cup (25g) cocoa powder
2 eggs
chocolate ganache
½ cup (125ml) cream
200g dark eating chocolate, chopped coarsely

1 Preheat oven to 160°C/140°C fan-forced. Grease deep 23cm-square cake pan; line base with baking paper.
2 Combine butter, sugar, milk, coffee, bourbon, extract and chocolate in medium saucepan; stir over low heat until smooth. Transfer to large bowl; cool 15 minutes. Whisk in sifted flours and cocoa then eggs.
3 Pour mixture into pan; bake about 1½ hours.
4 Stand cake 5 minutes before turning, top-side up, onto wire rack to cool.
5 Meanwhile, make ganache.
6 Spread cold cake with ganache.
chocolate ganache Bring cream to the boil in small saucepan. Remove from heat, add chocolate; stir until smooth. Stand 10 minutes before using.
nutritional count per serving 32.6g total fat (20.4g saturated fat); 2721kJ (651 cal); 78.7g carbohydrate; 6.3g protein; 1.3g fibre

preparation time 20 minutes (plus refrigeration and cooling time) | cooking time 40 minutes | makes 60

pistachio and cranberry biscotti

60g unsalted butter, softened
1 teaspoon vanilla extract
1 cup (220g) caster sugar
2 eggs
1¾ cups (260g) plain flour
½ teaspoon bicarbonate of soda
1 cup (130g) dried cranberries
¾ cup (110g) coarsely chopped
   roasted pistachios
1 egg, extra
1 tablespoon water
2 tablespoons caster sugar, extra

1 Beat butter, extract and sugar in medium bowl until combined. Beat in eggs, one at a time. Stir in sifted flours and soda then cranberries and nuts. Cover dough; refrigerate 1 hour.

2 Preheat oven to 180°C/160°C fan-forced. Grease oven tray.

3 Knead dough on floured surface until smooth but still sticky. Halve dough; shape each half into 30cm log. Place logs on oven tray.

4 Combine extra egg with the water in small bowl. Brush egg mixture over logs; sprinkle with extra sugar. Bake about 20 minutes or until firm; cool 3 hours or overnight.

5 Preheat oven to 160°C/140°C fan-forced.

6 Using serrated knife, cut logs diagonally into 1cm slices. Place slices on ungreased oven trays. Bake about 15 minutes or until dry and crisp, turning halfway through baking time; cool on wire racks.

nutritional count per piece *2.1g total fat (0.7g saturated fat); 259kJ (62 cal); 9.2g carbohydrate; 1.2g protein; 0.4g fibre*

preparation time 15 minutes | cooking time 20 minutes | makes 12

pear and almond friands

6 egg whites
185g butter, melted
1 cup (120g) almond meal
1½ cups (240g) icing sugar
¾ cup (110g) plain flour
1 small pear (180g), peeled, cored,
**   chopped finely**
¼ cup (20g) flaked almonds

1 Preheat oven to 200°C/180°C fan-forced. Grease 12-hole (⅓-cup/80ml) muffin pan.
2 Whisk egg whites in medium bowl until frothy. Add butter, meal, sifted icing sugar and flour, then pear; stir until combined.
3 Place ¼-cups of mixture into pan holes; sprinkle with nuts.
4 Bake about 20 minutes. Stand 5 minutes before turning, top-side up, onto wire rack to cool.
nutritional count per friand *19.2g total fat*
(8.8g saturated fat); 1300kJ (311 cal);
28.8g carbohydrate; 5.3g protein; 1.6g fibre

lemon and coconut friands

6 egg whites
185g butter, melted
1 cup (100g) hazelnut meal
1½ cups (240g) icing sugar
½ cup (75g) plain flour
2 teaspoons finely grated lemon rind
1 tablespoon lemon juice
¼ cup (20g) desiccated coconut
⅓ cup (15g) flaked coconut

1 Preheat oven to 200°C/180°C fan-forced.
Grease 12-hole (⅓-cup/80ml) muffin pan.
2 Whisk egg whites in medium bowl until frothy.
Add butter, meal, sifted icing sugar and flour, rind,
juice and desiccated coconut; stir until combined.
3 Place ¼-cups of mixture into pan holes; sprinkle
with flaked coconut.
4 Bake about 20 minutes. Stand 5 minutes before
turning, top-side up, onto wire rack to cool.
nutritional count per friand *19.7g total fat
(10.2g saturated fat); 1237kJ (296 cal);
25.3g carbohydrate; 4g protein; 1.6g fibre*

polenta and almond orange cake

2 medium oranges (480g)
⅔ cup (110g) roasted blanched almonds
¾ cup (165g) caster sugar
1 teaspoon baking powder
6 eggs
1 cup (120g) almond meal
1 cup (170g) polenta
50g butter, melted

1   Cover unpeeled whole oranges in medium saucepan with cold water, bring to the boil. Boil, uncovered, 30 minutes; drain. Repeat process with fresh water, boil about 1 hour or until oranges are tender; drain. Cool oranges.

2   Preheat oven to 200°C/180°C fan-forced. Grease deep 22cm-round cake pan; line base and side with baking paper.

3   Blend or process nuts with 1 tablespoon of the sugar until coarse.

4   Trim ends from oranges then cut in half; discard seeds. Blend or process oranges, including rind, with baking powder until mixture is pulpy.

5   Beat eggs with remaining sugar in small bowl with electric mixer until light and fluffy. Transfer to large bowl; fold in nut mixture, almond meal, polenta, butter and orange pulp.

6   Spread mixture into pan; bake about 50 minutes. Cool 5 minutes before turning cake, top-side up, onto serving plate; serve dusted with sifted icing sugar, if you like.

nutritional count per serving *17g total fat (3.8g saturated fat); 1271kJ (304 cal); 27.8g carbohydrate; 8.8g protein; 2.9g fibre*

preparation time 45 minutes | cooking time 25 minutes | makes 36

baklava cigars

1 cup (160g) blanched almonds
½ cup (70g) unsalted pistachios
1 teaspoon ground cinnamon
1 teaspoon ground nutmeg
½ teaspoon ground clove
1 cup (250ml) water
1 cup (220g) white sugar
1 teaspoon finely grated lemon rind
2 teaspoons rosewater
16 sheets fillo pastry
150g butter, melted

1 Preheat oven to 180°C/160°C fan-forced. Grease two oven trays.

2 Blend or process nuts and spices until finely chopped; spread mixture onto oven tray. Roast, about 10 minutes or until browned lightly.

3 Meanwhile, combine the water and sugar in small saucepan. Stir over heat, without boiling, until sugar dissolves; bring to the boil then simmer, uncovered, without stirring, about 5 minutes or until slightly thickened. Add rind and rosewater. Combine ¼ cup rosewater syrup with nut mixture in small bowl; reserve remaining syrup.

4 Increase oven to 220°C/200°C fan-forced.

5 Cut one pastry sheet crossways into three strips, brush each strip with butter (cover remaining pastry sheets with baking paper then damp tea towel). Spoon heaped teaspoon of nut mixture on one end of each strip, leaving 3.5cm border from short edge. Roll pastry tightly into cigar shape; brush with butter. Place on tray; cover with dry tea towel. Repeat with remaining pastry, butter and nut mixture. Bake cigars about 15 minutes.

6 Meanwhile, heat remaining syrup. Place cigars, in single layer, in large shallow dish; pour hot syrup over hot cigars. Cool in dish.

nutritional count per cigar *9.2g total fat (4.2g saturated fat); 573kJ (137 cal); 11.7g carbohydrate; 1.9g protein; 0.7g fibre*

preparation time 10 minutes | cooking time 10 minutes | makes 24

white chocolate macadamia cookies

1½ cups (225g) plain flour
½ teaspoon bicarbonate of soda
¼ cup (55g) caster sugar
⅓ cup (75g) firmly packed brown sugar
125g butter, melted
½ teaspoon vanilla extract
1 egg
180g white eating chocolate, chopped coarsely
¾ cup (105g) roasted macadamias,
    chopped coarsely

1   Preheat oven to 200°C/180°C fan-forced.
Grease two oven trays; line with baking paper.
2   Sift flour, soda and sugars into large bowl. Stir in
butter, extract and egg then chocolate and nuts.
3   Drop rounded tablespoons of mixture, 5cm apart
on trays. Bake about 10 minutes. Cool on trays.
nutritional count per cookie   *10.4g total fat*
(4.9g saturated fat); 706kJ (169 cal);
16.4g carbohydrate; 2.2g protein; 0.6g fibre

preparation time 15 minutes (plus refrigeration time) | cooking time 20 minutes | makes 28

almond and chocolate florentines

50g butter
¼ cup (55g) caster sugar
2 teaspoons honey
1 tablespoon plain flour
1 tablespoon cream
½ cup (40g) flaked almonds
50g dark cooking chocolate, melted

1 Preheat oven to 200°C/180°C fan-forced. Grease four oven trays. Line trays with baking paper.
2 Combine butter, sugar, honey, flour and cream in small saucepan; bring to the boil, stirring. Reduce heat; cook, without stirring, 2 minutes. Remove from heat; stir in nuts.
3 Drop level teaspoons of mixture about 8cm apart onto trays. Bake about 6 minutes or until golden brown. Remove from oven; using metal spatula, push florentines into rounds. Cool on trays 1 minute then carefully lift florentines onto baking-paper-lined wire rack to cool. Drizzle florentines with chocolate; refrigerate until set.
nutritional count per florentine *3.1g total fat (1.7g saturated fat); 188kJ (45 cal); 3.8g carbohydrate; 0.4g protein; 0.2g fibre*

lime curd tart

3 eggs
4 egg yolks
2 teaspoons finely grated lime rind
½ cup (125ml) lime juice
1 cup (220g) caster sugar
200g unsalted butter, chopped
1 cup (50g) flaked coconut

sweet pastry
1¼ cups (185g) plain flour
½ cup (80g) icing sugar
¼ cup (20g) desiccated coconut
125g cold unsalted butter
¼ cup (60ml) iced water, approximately

1   Make sweet pastry.

2   Grease 24cm-round loose-based flan tin. Roll pastry between sheets of baking paper until large enough to line tin. Ease pastry into tin, press into base and side; trim edge, prick base with fork. Cover; refrigerate 30 minutes.

3   Preheat oven to 200°C/180°C fan-forced.

4   Place tin on oven tray; cover pastry with baking paper, fill with dried beans or uncooked rice. Bake 15 minutes; remove paper and beans carefully from pastry case. Bake about 10 minutes; cool.

5   Meanwhile, combine eggs, yolks, rind, juice, sugar and butter in medium saucepan; stir over medium heat, without boiling, about 15 minutes or until mixture coats the back of a spoon. Strain lime curd through sieve into medium bowl; stand 10 minutes then pour into pastry case. Refrigerate 2 hours before serving sprinkled with coconut.

sweet pastry Process flour, sugar, coconut and butter until crumbly; add enough of the water to make ingredients come together. Knead dough gently on floured surface until smooth. Wrap in plastic; refrigerate 30 minutes.

nutritional count per serving *35.4g total fat (22.9g saturated fat); 2178kJ (521 cal); 44.2g carbohydrate; 6g protein; 1.8g fibre*

preparation time 10 minutes | cooking time 45 minutes | serves 8

ginger sticky date pudding

1 cup (140g) seeded dried dates
¼ cup (55g) glacé ginger
1 teaspoon bicarbonate of soda
1 cup (250ml) boiling water
50g butter, chopped
½ cup (110g) firmly packed brown sugar
2 eggs
1 cup (150g) self-raising flour
1 teaspoon ground ginger
butterscotch sauce
300ml cream
¾ cup (165g) firmly packed brown sugar
75g butter, chopped

1 Preheat oven to 200°C/180°C fan-forced. Grease deep 20cm-round cake pan; line base with baking paper.
2 Combine dates, ginger, soda and the water in food processor; stand 5 minutes then add butter and sugar. Process until mixture is almost smooth. Add eggs, flour and ginger; process until combined.
3 Pour mixture into pan; bake about 45 minutes. Stand 10 minutes before turning onto serving plate.
4 Meanwhile, make butterscotch sauce. Serve pudding warm with sauce.
butterscotch sauce Stir ingredients in medium saucepan over low heat until sauce is smooth.
nutritional count per serving *30.1g total fat (19.6g saturated fat); 2337kJ (559 cal); 65.1g carbohydrate; 4.7g protein; 2.4g fibre*

anise-flavoured shortbread

250g unsalted butter, softened
½ cup (80g) icing sugar
2 cups (300g) plain flour
½ cup (100g) rice flour
3 teaspoons ground aniseed

1 Beat butter and sifted icing sugar in medium bowl with electric mixer until light and fluffy. Add sifted flours and aniseed, in two batches, beating on low speed after each addition, only until combined. Knead on floured surface until smooth. Cover; refrigerate 1 hour.

2 Preheat oven to 160°C/140°C fan-forced. Grease three oven trays.

3 Roll dough between sheets of baking paper until 5mm thick. Cut 36 x 6cm rounds from dough; place on oven trays about 3cm apart. Refrigerate 15 minutes.

4 Bake biscuits about 12 minutes; cool on trays.

nutritional count per shortbread *5.9g total fat (3.8g saturated fat); 418kJ (100 cal); 10.5g carbohydrate; 1.1g protein; 0.4g fibre* preparation time 15 minutes (plus refrigeration time) | cooking time 5 minutes | makes 16

jaffa rocky road

3 slices (60g) glacé orange, chopped finely
200g white marshmallows, chopped coarsely
½ cup (70g) unsalted pistachios,
    chopped coarsely
250g milk eating chocolate, chopped coarsely
100g dark eating chocolate, chopped coarsely
60g butter

1 Grease deep 19cm-square cake pan; line
base and two opposite sides with baking paper,
extending paper 5cm above sides.
2 Combine orange, marshmallow and nuts in
large bowl. Stir chocolates and butter in medium
heatproof bowl, over medium saucepan of
simmering water until smooth.
3 Pour chocolate mixture over orange mixture;
stir until combined. Spoon rocky road mixture into
pan; refrigerate until set. Remove rocky road from
pan before cutting into squares.
nutritional count per piece *11.4g total fat*
(6g saturated fat); 932kJ (223 cal);
26.8g carbohydrate; 3g protein; 0.6g fibre

preparation time 45 minutes (plus refrigeration time) | cooking time 1 hour 10 minutes | serves 8

apple cranberry pie

Both Granny Smith and Golden Delicious apples are suitable for this recipe.

2 cups (300g) plain flour
150g cold unsalted butter, chopped coarsely
½ cup (125ml) iced water
1 egg
1 tablespoon milk
1 tablespoon caster sugar

cranberry filling
½ cup (110g) caster sugar
2 tablespoons water
300g frozen cranberries

apple filling
10 medium apples (1.5kg)
½ cup (125ml) water
⅓ cup (75g) caster sugar

1 Process flour and butter until crumbly; add enough of the water to bring ingredients together. Press dough into a ball. Cover; refrigerate 1 hour.

2 Make cranberry filling. Make apple filling.

3 Preheat oven to 220°C/200°C fan-forced.

4 Divide pastry in half. Roll half between sheets of baking paper until large enough to line deep 25cm pie dish; lift pastry into dish. Spoon cranberry filling into pastry case; top with apple filling. Bring edge of pastry case up over filling; brush pastry edge with combined egg and milk.

5 Roll remaining pastry until large enough to cover top of pie; press edges together with fork to seal. Brush with egg mixture; sprinkle with sugar. Bake 15 minutes. Reduce oven to 180°C/160°C fan-forced; bake 30 minutes.

cranberry filling Combine sugar, the water and cranberries in medium saucepan; simmer, stirring, about 10 minutes or until syrupy. Remove from heat; cool.

apple filling Peel, quarter, core and slice apples thinly; combine in large saucepan with the water. Simmer, stirring occasionally, about 10 minutes or until apple is tender. Drain apple; discard liquid. Stir sugar into apple; cool.

nutritional count per serving 16.8g total fat (10.5g saturated fat); 1981kJ (474 cal); 72.2g carbohydrate; 5.7g protein; 4.9g fibre

chocolate raspberry tart

¾ cup (240g) raspberry jam
200g dark eating chocolate, chopped finely
25g unsalted butter, melted
⅔ cup (160ml) cream, warmed
120g raspberries
sweet pastry
1¼ cups (185g) plain flour
½ cup (80g) icing sugar
125g cold unsalted butter, chopped coarsely
¼ cup (60ml) iced water, approximately

1 Make sweet pastry.
2 Grease 12.5cm x 35cm (or 24cm-round) loose-based flan tin. Roll pastry between sheets of baking paper until large enough to line tin. Ease pastry into tin, press into base and side; trim edge, prick base with fork. Cover; refrigerate 30 minutes.
3 Preheat oven to 200°C/180°C fan-forced.
4 Place tin on oven tray; cover pastry with baking paper, fill with dried beans or uncooked rice. Bake 15 minutes; remove paper and beans carefully from pastry case. Bake about 10 minutes. Spread jam over pastry base; return to oven 2 minutes. Cool.
5 Combine chocolate, butter and cream in medium bowl; whisk until smooth. Pour chocolate mixture into pastry case; refrigerate 2 hours. Top tart with raspberries.
sweet pastry Process flour, icing sugar and butter until crumbly; add enough of the water to make ingredients come together. Knead dough gently on floured surface until smooth. Wrap in plastic; refrigerate 30 minutes.
nutritional count per serving *21g total fat (13.4g saturated fat); 1559kJ (373 cal); 42.4g carbohydrate; 3g protein; 1.6g fibre*

preparation time 15 minutes | cooking time 25 minutes | makes 9

hazelnut brownies

125g butter
200g dark eating chocolate
½ cup (110g) caster sugar
2 eggs, beaten lightly
1¼ cups (185g) plain flour
½ cup (70g) roasted hazelnuts, chopped coarsely
1 cup (190g) white Choc Bits

1   Preheat oven to 180°C/160°C fan-forced.
Grease deep 19cm-square cake pan; line base
and two opposite sides with baking paper,
extending paper 5cm above sides.
2   Melt butter and chocolate in medium saucepan
over low heat. Stir in sugar; cook, stirring, 5 minutes.
Cool 10 minutes.
3   Stir in egg and sifted flour then nuts and
Choc Bits. Spread mixture into pan. Bake about
30 minutes. Cool in pan before cutting into squares.
Serve dusted with icing sugar, if you like.
nutritional count per brownie *30g total fat*
(15.5g saturated fat); 2174kJ (520 cal);
54.7g carbohydrate; 7.2g protein; 2.1g fibre

blueberry crumble

You can use fresh or frozen blueberries for
this recipe, or a combination of both.

¼ cup (55g) brown sugar
¼ cup (55g) caster sugar
¾ cup (110g) plain flour
1 teaspoon ground cinnamon
100g butter, chopped coarsely
¾ cup (65g) rolled oats
½ cup (70g) coarsely chopped
   roasted macadamias
500g blueberries
1 tablespoon lemon juice
¼ cup (55g) caster sugar, extra

1 Preheat oven to 200°C/180°C fan-forced.
2 Sift sugars, flour and cinnamon into medium
bowl; rub in butter. Stir in oats and nuts.
3 Combine blueberries with juice and extra sugar
in medium bowl.
4 Divide blueberry mixture among four 1-cup
(250ml) ovenproof dishes; sprinkle with crumble
topping. Bake about 40 minutes. Serve with
vanilla ice-cream, if you like.
nutritional count per serving *35.7g total fat
(15.6g saturated fat); 2939kJ (703 cal);
85.9g carbohydrate; 7g protein; 5.5g fibre*

carrot cupcakes with maple frosting

You need four medium carrots for this recipe.

½ cup (125ml) vegetable oil
3 eggs
1½ cups (225g) self-raising flour
1 cup (220g) firmly packed brown sugar
2 teaspoons mixed spice
2 cups (480g) firmly packed
    coarsely grated carrot
¾ cup (90g) coarsely chopped roasted pecans
6 roasted pecans, halved
maple cream cheese frosting
30g butter, softened
80g cream cheese, softened
2 tablespoons maple syrup
1¼ cups (200g) icing sugar

1 Preheat oven to 180°C/160°C fan-forced. Line 12-hole (⅓-cup/80ml) muffin pan with paper cases.
2 Stir oil, eggs, sifted flour, sugar and spice in medium bowl until combined. Stir in carrot and chopped nuts.
3 Divide mixture among paper cases; bake about 30 minutes. Stand cupcakes 5 minutes before turning, top-side up, onto wire rack to cool.
4 Meanwhile, make maple cream cheese frosting. Spread frosting over cupcakes; top each with a nut.
maple cream cheese frosting Beat butter, cream cheese and syrup in small bowl with electric mixer until light and fluffy; gradually beat in sifted icing sugar until frosting is spreadable.
nutritional count per cupcake *22.4g total fat (4.8g saturated fat); 1848kJ (442 cal); 53.4g carbohydrate; 5.4g protein; 2.9g fibre*

baked cheesecake with liqueur cherries

We used a mixture of 90g shredded wheatmeal biscuits and 90g morning coffee biscuits for this crust.

180g plain sweet biscuits
125g butter, melted
500g cream cheese, softened
250g mascarpone, softened
1 cup (220g) caster sugar
2 teaspoons finely grated lemon rind
2 teaspoons vanilla extract
3 eggs

liqueur cherries
300g frozen cherries
2 tablespoons kirsch
1 tablespoon water
1 tablespoon caster sugar
1 teaspoon lemon juice

1 Grease 24cm springform tin; line side with baking paper.
2 Blend or process biscuits until fine. Add butter; blend until combined. Press mixture over base of tin; place tin on oven tray, refrigerate 30 minutes.
3 Preheat oven to 200°C/180°C fan-forced.
4 Bake crumb crust, on tray, 10 minutes; cool.
5 Reduce oven to 180°C/160°C fan-forced.
6 Beat cream cheese, mascarpone, sugar, rind and extract in medium bowl with electric mixer until smooth. Beat in eggs, one at a time. Do not overbeat.
7 Pour filling into crust; bake 50 minutes. Cool cheesecake in oven with door ajar. Cover; refrigerate 3 hours or overnight.
8 Make liqueur cherries. Top cheesecake with liqueur cherries before serving.

liqueur cherries Combine ingredients in medium saucepan; bring to the boil. Reduce heat; simmer about 10 minutes or until mixture is slightly thickened.

nutritional count per serving *36g total fat (22.8g saturated fat); 2111kJ (505 cal); 36.2g carbohydrate; 7.5g protein; 0.7g fibre*

preparation time 20 minutes (plus cooling time) | cooking time 50 minutes | serves 6

plum clafoutis

If plums are not in season, use a 1kg jar of whole plums. Drain, halve and seed them before using.

10 small plums (750g), halved, seeded
1 cinnamon stick, halved
¼ cup (60ml) water
¼ cup (55g) brown sugar
⅔ cup (160ml) milk
⅔ cup (160ml) cream
1 teaspoon vanilla extract
4 eggs
½ cup (110g) caster sugar
¼ cup (35g) plain flour

1 Preheat oven to 200°C/180°C fan-forced. Grease shallow 2.5-litre (10-cup) ovenproof dish.
2 Place plums in medium baking dish with cinnamon and the water; sprinkle with sugar. Cook about 15 minutes or until plums soften.
3 Remove cinnamon from dish and add to medium saucepan with milk, cream and extract; bring to the boil. Cool; remove cinnamon stick.
4 Whisk eggs and sugar in medium bowl until light and frothy; whisk in flour then whisk mixture into cream mixture.
5 Place drained plums in shallow ovenproof dish; pour cream mixture over plums. Bake about 30 minutes or until browned lightly. Serve dusted with icing sugar, if you like.

nutritional count per serving *16.1g total fat (9.3g saturated fat); 1417kJ (339 cal); 46.2g carbohydrate; 7.1g protein; 2.4g fibre*

preparation time 20 minutes | cooking time 10 minutes | serves 4

banana split

4 medium bananas (800g), halved lengthways
2 tablespoons brown sugar
100g dark eating chocolate
300ml thickened cream
1 tablespoon dark rum
4 scoops (240ml) vanilla ice-cream
4 scoops (240ml) chocolate ice-cream
⅔ cup (80g) coarsely chopped roasted pecans
⅓ cup (25g) toasted shredded coconut

1 Preheat grill.
2 Place bananas, cut-sides up, on oven tray;
sprinkle with sugar. Grill about 3 minutes or until
sugar melts.
3 Meanwhile, melt chocolate with 2 tablespoons
of the cream in small bowl set over small saucepan
of simmering water.
4 Beat remaining cream with rum in small bowl
with electric mixer until soft peaks form.
5 Place 2 banana halves in each of four dishes;
top each with a scoop of the vanilla and chocolate
ice-cream. Top each with cream; drizzle with
chocolate then sprinkle with nuts and coconut.
nutritional count per serving *60.1g total fat
(31.7g saturated fat); 3618kJ (865 cal);
65.7g carbohydrate; 9.9g protein; 5.8g fibre*

preparation time 1 hour (plus cooling time) | cooking time 1 hour 15 minutes | makes 36

lamingtons

If you don't want to make this cake, you could make or buy a basic sponge or buttercake.

250g butter, softened
2 cups (440g) caster sugar
6 eggs
¾ cup (180g) sour cream
2 cups (300g) plain flour
¼ cup (35g) self-raising flour
2½ cups (200g) desiccated coconut
chocolate icing
4 cups (500g) icing sugar
½ cup (50g) cocoa powder
20g butter, melted
⅔ cup (160ml) milk

1   Preheat oven to 160°C/140°C fan-forced. Grease deep 23cm-square cake pan; line base with baking paper.
2   Beat butter and sugar in large bowl with electric mixer until light and fluffy. Beat in eggs, one at a time. (Mixture might separate at this stage but will come together later.) Stir in sour cream and sifted flours, in two batches.
3   Spread mixture into pan; bake about 55 minutes. Stand 10 minutes before turning, top-side up, onto wire rack to cool.
4   Meanwhile, make chocolate icing.
5   Trim cold cake so top is level; cut into 36 squares. Dip squares in icing, drain off excess then coat in coconut; place lamingtons on wire rack to set.
chocolate icing Sift icing sugar and cocoa into large heatproof bowl; stir in butter and milk. Stir icing over large saucepan of simmering water until it is of a coating consistency.

nutritional count per lamington *13.1g total fat (9.1g saturated fat); 1120kJ (268 cal); 33.9g carbohydrate; 3g protein; 1.2g fibre*

glossary

ALMONDS flat, pointy-tipped nuts with a pitted brown shell enclosing a creamy white kernel that is covered by a brown skin.
meal also known as ground almonds; nuts are powdered to a coarse flour texture for use in baking or as a thickening agent.

AIOLI homemade garlic mayonnaise originally from the south of France.

ANISE SEED also known as aniseed; a licorice-tasting seed from a feathery plant. Do not confuse with the star anise used in Asian cooking.

BAY LEAVES aromatic leaves from the bay tree; available fresh or dried. Used to add a strong, slightly peppery flavour to soups, stocks and casseroles.

BEANS
black-eyed also known as black-eyed peas or cowpeas; the dried seed of a variant of the snake (or yard-long) bean. Not too dissimilar to white beans in flavour.
cannellini small white bean similar in appearance and flavour to great northern, navy and haricot beans.

BEETROOT also known as red beets; a firm, round root vegetable. Can be grated or finely chopped; boiled or steamed then diced or sliced; or roasted then mashed.

BICARBONATE OF SODA also known as baking soda.

BLINI also known as blintzes; yeast-risen buckwheat pancakes. Originally from Russia and are traditionally served with sour cream and caviar or smoked salmon.

BRIOCHE French in origin; a rich, yeast-leavened, cake-like bread made with butter and eggs. Most common form is the brioche à tête, a round fluted roll topped with a much smaller ball of dough. Eaten freshly baked or toasted; available from cake or specialty bread shops.

BRUSCHETTA pronounced broo-skeh-tah; this traditional Italian snack is fresh white bread, usually ciabatta, rubbed with garlic-infused olive oil, toasted and served with various toppings.

BUCKWHEAT FLOUR used for making blini, pancakes and soba noodles; ground from a herb belonging to the same plant family as rhubarb; not a cereal so is gluten-free.

BUTTERMILK originally the term given to the slightly sour liquid left after butter was churned from cream, today it is commercially made similarly to yogurt. Sold alongside fresh milk products in supermarkets. Despite the implication of its name, buttermilk is low in fat.

CAPSICUM also known as pepper or bell pepper. Available in green, yellow, orange, purplish-black and red varieties. Discard seeds and membranes before use.

CHEESE
bocconcini from the diminutive of "boccone", meaning mouthful in Italian; a walnut-sized, baby mozzarella. Is a delicate, semi-soft, white cheese traditionally made from buffalo milk. Sold fresh, it spoils rapidly so will only keep, refrigerated in brine, for one or two days at most.
cream commonly known as philadelphia or philly; a soft cow-milk cheese.
fetta Greek in origin; a crumbly textured goat- or sheep-milk cheese having a sharp, salty taste. Ripened and stored in salted whey.
goat made from goats milk, has a strong, earthy taste. Available in soft, crumbly and firm textures, in various shapes and sizes, and sometimes rolled in ash or herbs.
gruyère a hard-rind swiss cheese with small holes and a nutty, slightly salty flavour.
haloumi a Greek Cypriot cheese having a semi-firm, spongy texture and a very salty, yet sweet, flavour. Ripened and stored in salted whey; it's best grilled or fried, and holds its shape well on being heated. Should be eaten while still warm as it becomes tough and rubbery on cooling.
mozzarella soft, spun-curd, cow-milk cheese; it is the most popular pizza cheese because of its low melting point and elasticity when heated.

parmesan also known as parmigiano; is a hard, grainy cow-milk cheese. The curd is salted in brine for a month then aged for up to two years.
roquefort considered the "king of cheeses", this is a blue cheese with a singularly pungent taste; made only from the milk of specially bred sheep and ripened in the damp limestone caves found under the village of Roquefort-sur-Soulzon in France. Has a sticky, bone-coloured rind and, when ripe, the sharp, almost metallic-tasting interior is creamy and almost shiny. It is one of the world's best eating cheeses and is most famously used in the self-named salad dressing.
ricotta a soft, sweet, moist, white cow-milk cheese with a low-fat content and a slightly grainy texture. The name roughly translates as "cooked again" and refers to ricotta's manufacture from a whey that is itself a by-product of other cheese making.
taleggio an Italian smooth, firm, cow-milk cheese having a creamy, nutty taste and brown or red rind; an ideal melting or grilling cheese. Can be used similarly to another soft Italian cheese, fontina.

CHICKPEAS also called channa, garbanzos or hummus; a sandy-coloured, irregularly round legume. Available canned or dried (the latter needs several hours reconstituting in cold water before being used).

CHORIZO sausage of Spanish origin, made of coarsely ground pork and highly seasoned with garlic and chilli.

COCOA POWDER also known as unsweetened cocoa; fermented, roasted, ground cocoa beans.

CORNFLOUR also known as cornstarch. Available made from corn or wheat; used as a thickening agent in cooking.

CORNICHON French for gherkin; a small variety of pickled cucumber.

CRANBERRIES available dried and frozen; have a rich, astringent flavour and can be used in cooking sweet or savoury dishes. The dried version can usually be substituted for or with other dried fruit.

FINES HERBES pronounced fin-erb, this is a french seasoning mixture made up of fresh chervil, flat-leafed parsley, chives and tarragon; its crisp, clean flavour makes it a welcome addition to simple white sauces, omelettes, stocks and soups.

FIVE-SPICE POWDER also known as chinese five-spice. Is usually a fragrant mixture of star anise, ground cinnamon, fennel seeds, sichuan pepper and cloves.

FLOUR
plain also known as all-purpose; unbleached wheat flour is the best for baking: the gluten content ensures a strong dough, which produces a light result. Also used as a thickening agent.
self-raising all-purpose plain or wholemeal flour with baking powder added; can be made at home with plain or wholemeal flour sifted with baking powder in the proportion of 1 cup flour to 2 teaspoons baking powder.

FRENCH GREEN LENTILS a local cousin to the famous (and very expensive) French lentils du puy; green-blue, tiny lentils with a nutty, earthy flavour and a hardy nature so they can be rapidly cooked without disintegrating.

GANACHE pronounced gah-nash, a delicious creamy chocolate filling or frosting for cakes. Depending on its use, it is made from varying proportions of good-quality chocolate and pouring cream. Other ingredients can be added for flavour or to increase its richness or gloss. Ganache can be whipped, piped or poured like a glaze, and can be frozen for up to 3 months.

HAZELNUTS also known as filberts; plump, grape-size, rich, sweet nut having a brown inedible skin that is removed by rubbing heated nuts together vigorously in a tea towel.
meal hazelnuts that have been ground into a coarse flour texture.

HOISIN SAUCE a thick, sweet and spicy Chinese barbecue sauce made from salted fermented soy beans, onions and garlic; used as a marinade or baste.

HORSERADISH available bottled in two forms: prepared horseradish, the unadulterated preserved grated root; and horseradish cream, a commercially prepared creamy paste consisting of grated horseradish, vinegar, oil and sugar. These cannot be substituted one for the other in cooking, but both can be used as table condiments.

HUMMUS a Middle-Eastern salad or dip made from softened dried chickpeas, garlic, lemon juice and tahini (sesame-seed paste); can be purchased ready-made from most delicatessens and supermarkets.

JALAPEÑO pronounced hah-lah-pain-yo. Fairly hot, medium-sized, plump, dark green chilli; available fresh or pickled, and canned or bottled from greengrocers.

JAM also known as preserve or conserve; a thickened mixture of a fruit and sugar.

KIRSCH German for "cherry water"; kirsch is a colourless brandy made from a double distillation of the fermented juice of sour morello cherries. An essential ingredient in many popular cocktails, and in a classic Swiss fondue, as well as the German black forest cake and other chocolate desserts.

KIWIFRUIT also known as chinese gooseberry; having a brown, somewhat hairy skin and bright-green or yellow flesh with a unique sweet-tart flavour. Used in fruit salads, desserts and eaten (peeled) as is.

KUMARA the Polynesian name of an orange-fleshed sweet potato often confused with yam; good baked, boiled, mashed or fried similarly to other potatoes.

KORMA PASTE a classic North Indian sauce with a rich yet delicate coconut flavour; usually includes cinnamon, cumin, fennel, mace, garlic, ginger and coriander.

LAMINGTON PAN 20cm x 30cm slab cake pan, 3cm deep.

LEEK member of the onion family used more often in cooking than eaten on its own. Looks like a large green onion; has a mild flavour.

LETTUCE
butter small, round, loosely formed head with sweet, soft, buttery-textured leaves.
cos also known as romaine lettuce; the traditional caesar salad lettuce. The long leaves have a stiff centre rib that gives a slight cupping effect to the leaf on either side.
iceberg a heavy, firm, round lettuce with tightly packed leaves and a crisp texture; the most common "family" lettuce used on sandwiches and in salads.
oak leaf also known as feuille de chene; curly-leafed lettuce. Found in red and green varieties.
radicchio Italian in origin; a member of the chicory family. The dark burgundy leaves and strong, bitter flavour can be cooked or eaten raw in salads.

LIGHT SOY SAUCE light in colour with a fairly thin consistency; slightly saltier than other varieties. Used in dishes in which the natural or original colour of the ingredients is to be maintained. It shouldn't be confused with salt-reduced or low-sodium products.

MAPLE SYRUP distilled from the sap of maple trees. Maple-flavoured syrup or pancake syrup is not an adequate substitute for the real thing.

MESCLUN pronounced mess-kluhn; also known as mixed greens or spring salad mix. A commercial blend of assorted young lettuce and other green leaves, including baby spinach leaves, mizuna and curly endive.

MIZUNA Japanese in origin; the frizzy green salad leaves have a delicate mustard flavour.

MUESLI also known as granola; a combination of grains (mainly oats), nuts and dried fruits.

MUSHROOMS
button small, cultivated white mushrooms with a mild flavour. When a recipe in this book calls for an unspecified type of mushroom, use button.
oyster also known as abalone; grey-white mushrooms shaped like a fan. Prized for their smooth texture and subtle, oyster-like flavour.

shiitake when fresh, these are also known as chinese black, forest or golden oak mushrooms. Although cultivated, they have the earthiness and taste of wild mushrooms. Large and meaty, they can be used as a substitute for meat in some Asian vegetarian dishes. When dried, they are known as donko or dried chinese mushrooms; have a unique meaty flavour and must be rehydrated before use.

swiss brown also known as roman or cremini. Light to dark brown mushrooms with full-bodied flavour; suited for use in casseroles or being stuffed and baked.

MUSTARD

american-style bright yellow in colour, a sweet mustard containing mustard seeds, sugar, salt, spices and garlic. Serve with hot dogs and hamburgers.

dijon also known as french mustard. Pale brown, creamy, distinctively flavoured, fairly mild mustard. Use in salad dressings.

wholegrain also known as seeded. A French-style coarse-grain mustard made from crushed mustard seeds and dijon-style mustard. Works well with cold meats and sausages.

POLENTA a flour-like cereal made of dried corn (maize) and sold ground in different textures; also known as cornmeal. Also the name of the dish made from it.

PRESERVED LEMONS whole or quartered salted lemons preserved in a mixture of olive oil and lemon juice; a North African specialty, they are usually added to casseroles and tagines to impart a rich, salty-sour acidic flavour. Available from delicatessens and specialty food shops. Use the rind only and rinse well under cold water before using.

PROSCIUTTO one variety of many different unsmoked Italian hams; salted, air-cured and aged, it is usually eaten uncooked. There are many styles of prosciutto, one of the best being Parma ham, from Italy's Emilia Romagna region, traditionally lightly salted, dried then eaten raw.

RICE

arborio small, round-grained rice able to absorb a large amount of liquid; the high level of starch makes it especially suitable for risottos.

basmati a white, fragrant long-grained rice; the grains fluff up beautifully when cooked. Wash several times before cooking.

RICE PAPER ROUNDS also known as banh trang; made from rice flour and water then stamped into rounds; quite brittle and break easily. Dipped briefly in water, they become pliable wrappers for food.

RICE VERMICELLI also known as sen mee, mei fun or bee hoon. Used throughout Asia in spring rolls and cold salads; a long thin noodle made with rice flour.

ROCKET a peppery green salad leaf also known as arugula, rugula and rucola. Baby rocket leaves are smaller and less peppery.

ROSEWATER an extract made from crushed rose petals, called gulab in India; used for its aromatic quality in many desserts.

SICHUAN PEPPERCORNS also known as szechuan or chinese pepper; native to the Sichuan province of China. Although not related to the peppercorn family, the small, red-brown sichuan berries look like black peppercorns and have a distinctive peppery-lemon flavour and aroma.

SILVER BEET also known as swiss chard and, incorrectly, spinach; has fleshy stalks and large, dark-green crinkly leaves.

STAR ANISE a dried star-shaped pod; the seeds have an astringent aniseed flavour.

SUGAR

caster also known as superfine or finely granulated table sugar.

icing pulverised granulated sugar crushed together with a small amount of cornflour.

palm also known as nam tan pip, jaggery, jawa or gula melaka; made from the sap of the sugar palm tree. Light brown to black in colour and usually sold in rock-hard cakes; substitute with brown sugar if unavailable.

pure icing also known as powdered or confectioners' sugar.

white coarse, granulated table sugar also known as crystal sugar.

SUMAC a purple-red, astringent spice ground from berries growing on shrubs that flourish wild around the Mediterranean; adds a tart, lemony flavour to dips and dressings and goes well with barbecued meat. Can be found in Middle-Eastern food stores.

TAPENADE a thick paste made from black or green olives, capers, anchovies, olive oil and lemon juice.

TOMATO

cherry also known as tiny tim or tom thumb tomatoes; a small, round tomato.

egg also called plum or roma, these are smallish, oval-shaped tomatoes much used in Italian cooking or salads.

grape small, long oval-shaped tomatoes with a good tomato flavour. Are often used whole in salads or eaten as a snack.

TORTILLA an unleavened, thin round bread originating in Mexico; available frozen, fresh or vacuum-packed. Two kinds are available: one made from wheat flour and the other from corn.

TURKISH BREAD also known as pide. Sold in long (about 45cm) flat loaves as well as individual rounds; made from wheat flour and sprinkled with black onion seeds (kalonji).

VANILLA

bean paste a handy alternative to using whole vanilla beans in cooking; made by blending pure vanilla concentrated extract and vanilla beans (including seeds) in an all natural sugar syrup. Available from specialty spice shops and gourmet food stores.

extract obtained from vanilla beans infused in water; a non-alcoholic version of essence.

ZUCCHINI also known as courgette; small, pale- or dark-green, yellow or white vegetable belonging to the squash family. Harvested when young, its edible flowers can be stuffed then deep-fried or oven-baked to make a delicious appetiser.

conversion chart

MEASURES

One Australian metric measuring cup holds approximately 250ml; one Australian metric tablespoon holds 20ml; one Australian metric teaspoon holds 5ml.

The difference between one country's measuring cups and another's is within a two- or three-teaspoon variance, and will not affect your cooking results. North America, New Zealand and the United Kingdom use a 15ml tablespoon.

All cup and spoon measurements are level. The most accurate way of measuring dry ingredients is to weigh them. When measuring liquids, use a clear glass or plastic jug with the metric markings.

We use large eggs with an average weight of 60g.

DRY MEASURES

METRIC	IMPERIAL
15g	½oz
30g	1oz
60g	2oz
90g	3oz
125g	4oz (¼lb)
155g	5oz
185g	6oz
220g	7oz
250g	8oz (½lb)
280g	9oz
315g	10oz
345g	11oz
375g	12oz (¾lb)
410g	13oz
440g	14oz
470g	15oz
500g	16oz (1lb)
750g	24oz (1½lb)
1kg	32oz (2lb)

OVEN TEMPERATURES

These oven temperatures are only a guide for conventional ovens. For fan-forced ovens, check the manufacturer's manual.

	°C (CELSIUS)	°F (FAHRENHEIT)	GAS MARK
Very slow	120	250	½
Slow	150	275-300	1-2
Moderately slow	160	325	3
Moderate	180	350-375	4-5
Moderately hot	200	400	6
Hot	220	425-450	7-8
Very hot	240	475	9

LIQUID MEASURES

METRIC	IMPERIAL
30ml	1 fluid oz
60ml	2 fluid oz
100ml	3 fluid oz
125ml	4 fluid oz
150ml	5 fluid oz (¼ pint/1 gill)
190ml	6 fluid oz
250ml	8 fluid oz
300ml	10 fluid oz (½ pint)
500ml	16 fluid oz
600ml	20 fluid oz (1 pint)
1000ml (1 litre)	1¾ pints

LENGTH MEASURES

METRIC	IMPERIAL
3mm	⅛ in
6mm	¼in
1cm	½in
2cm	¾in
2.5cm	1in
5cm	2in
6cm	2½in
8cm	3in
10cm	4in
13cm	5in
15cm	6in
18cm	7in
20cm	8in
23cm	9in
25cm	10in
28cm	11in
30cm	12in (1ft)

index

ARE YOU MISSING SOME COOKBOOKS?

The Australian Women's Weekly Cookbooks are available from bookshops, cookshops, supermarkets and other stores all over the world. You can also buy direct from the publisher, using the order form below.

TITLE	RRP	QTY	TITLE	RRP	QTY
100 Fast Fillets	£6.99		Grills	£6.99	
A Taste of Chocolate	£6.99		Indian Cooking Class	£6.99	
After Work Fast	£6.99		Japanese Cooking Class	£6.99	
Beginners Cooking Class	£6.99		Just For One	£6.99	
Beginners Thai	£6.99		Just For Two	£6.99	
Best Food Fast	£6.99		Kids' Birthday Cakes	£6.99	
Breads & Muffins	£6.99		Kids Cooking	£6.99	
Brunches, Lunches & Treats	£6.99		Kids' Cooking Step-by-Step	£6.99	
Cafe Classics	£6.99		Low-carb, Low-fat	£6.99	
Cafe Favourites	£6.99		Low-fat Food for Life	£6.99	
Cakes Bakes & Desserts	£6.99		Low-fat Meals in Minutes	£6.99	
Cakes Biscuits & Slices	£6.99		Main Course Salads	£6.99	
Cakes Cooking Class	£6.99		Mexican	£6.99	
Caribbean Cooking	£6.99		Middle Eastern Cooking Class	£6.99	
Casseroles	£6.99		Mince in Minutes	£6.99	
Casseroles & Slow-Cooked Classics	£6.99		Moroccan & the Foods of North Africa	£6.99	
Cheap Eats	£6.99		Muffins, Scones & Breads	£6.99	
Cheesecakes: baked and chilled	£6.99		New Casseroles	£6.99	
Chicken	£6.99		New Curries	£6.99	
Chicken Meals in Minutes	£6.99		New Finger Food	£6.99	
Chinese and the foods of Thailand, Vietnam, Malaysia & Japan	£6.99		New French Food	£6.99	
			New Salads	£6.99	
Chinese Cooking Class	£6.99		Party Food and Drink	£6.99	
Christmas Cooking	£6.99		Pasta Meals in Minutes	£6.99	
Chocs & Treats	£6.99		Potatoes	£6.99	
Cocktails	£6.99		Quick & Simple Cooking (Apr 08)	£6.99	
Cookies & Biscuits	£6.99		Rice & Risotto	£6.99	
Cooking Class Cake Decorating	£6.99		Sauces Salsas & Dressings	£6.99	
Cupcakes & Fairycakes	£6.99		Sensational Stir-Fries	£6.99	
Detox	£6.99		Simple Healthy Meals	£6.99	
Dinner Lamb	£6.99		Simple Starters Mains & Puds	£6.99	
Easy Comfort Food (May 08)	£6.99		Soup	£6.99	
Easy Curry	£6.99		Stir-fry	£6.99	
Easy Midweek Meals	£6.99		Superfoods for Exam Success	£6.99	
Easy Spanish-Style	£6.99		Tapas Mezze Antipasto & other bites	£6.99	
Food for Fit and Healthy Kids	£6.99		Thai Cooking Class	£6.99	
Foods of the Mediterranean	£6.99		Traditional Italian	£6.99	
Foods That Fight Back	£6.99		Vegetarian Meals in Minutes	£6.99	
Fresh Food Fast	£6.99		Vegie Food	£6.99	
Fresh Food for Babies & Toddlers	£6.99		Wicked Sweet Indulgences	£6.99	
Good Food for Babies & Toddlers	£6.99		Wok Meals in Minutes	£6.99	
Great Kids' Cakes (May 08)	£6.99				
Greek Cooking Class	£6.99		TOTAL COST:	£	

Mr/Mrs/Ms _____

Address_____ Postcode _____

Day time phone _____ email* (optional)_____

I enclose my cheque/money order for £ _____

or please charge £ _____

to my: ☐ Access ☐ Mastercard ☐ Visa ☐ Diners Club

Card number ☐☐☐☐ ☐☐☐☐ ☐☐☐☐ ☐☐☐☐ ☐☐☐☐

Expiry date _____ 3 digit security code *(found on reverse of card)* _____

Cardholder's name_____ Signature _____

To order: Mail or fax – photocopy or complete the order form above, and send your credit card details or cheque payable to: Australian Consolidated Press (UK), ACP Books, 10 Scirocco Close, Moulton Park Office Village, Northampton NN3 6AP. phone (+44) (0)1604 642200 fax (+44) (0)1604 642300 email books@acpuk.com or order online at www.acpuk.com
Non-UK residents: We accept the credit cards listed on the coupon, or cheques, drafts or International Money Orders payable in sterling and drawn on a UK bank. Credit card charges are at the exchange rate current at the time of payment. **Postage and packing UK:** Add £1.00 per order plus £1.75 per book. **Postage and packing overseas:** Add £2.00 per order plus £3.50 per book. All pricing current at time of going to press and subject to change/availability. **Offer ends 31.12.2008**

* By including your email address, you consent to receipt of any email regarding this magazine, and other emails which inform you of ACP's other publications, products and services, and to promote third party goods and services you may be interested in.

TEST KITCHEN
Food director Pamela Clark
Food editors Karen Hammial and Alexandra Somerville
Test Kitchen manager Kellie-Marie Thomas
Home economist Nancy Duran
Nutritional information Belinda Farlow

ACP BOOKS
General manager Christine Whiston
Editorial director Susan Tomnay
Creative director & designer Hieu Chi Nguyen
Senior editor Wendy Bryant
Director of sales Brian Cearnes
Marketing manager Bridget Cody
Business analyst Ashley Davies
Operations manager David Scotto
International rights enquires Laura Bamford
lbamford@acpuk.com

ACP Books are published by ACP Magazines a division of PBL Media Pty Limited
Group publisher, Women's lifestyle
Pat Ingram
Director of sales, Women's lifestyle
Lynette Phillips
Commercial manager, Women's lifestyle
Seymour Cohen
Marketing director, Women's lifestyle
Matthew Dominello
Public relations manager, Women's lifestyle
Hannah Deveraux
Creative director, Events, Women's lifestyle
Luke Bonnano
Research Director, Women's lifestyle
Justin Stone
ACP Magazines, Chief Executive officer
Scott Lorson
PBL Media, Chief Executive officer
Ian Law

Produced by ACP Books, Sydney.
Published by ACP Books, a division of ACP Magazines Ltd, 54 Park St, Sydney; GPO Box 4088, Sydney, NSW 2001. phone (02) 9282 8618 fax (02) 9267 9438. acpbooks@acpmagazines.com.au www.acpbooks.com.au
Printed by Dai Nippon in Korea.

Australia Distributed by Network Services, phone +61 2 9282 8777 fax +61 2 9264 3278 networkweb@networkservicescompany.com.au
United Kingdom Distributed by Australian Consolidated Press (UK), phone (01604) 642 200 fax (01604) 642 300 books@acpuk.com
New Zealand Distributed by Netlink Distribution Company, phone (9) 366 9966 ask@ndc.co.nz
South Africa Distributed by PSD Promotions, phone (27 11) 392 6065/6/7 fax (27 11) 392 6079/80 orders@psdprom.co.za

Cafe Favourites: The Australian Women's Weekly. Includes index.
ISBN 978 1 86396 742 6 (pbk).
1. Cookery. 2. Snack foods.
I. Clark, Pamela. II Title: Australian women's weekly 641.53
© ACP Magazines Ltd 2008
ABN 18 053 273 546
This publication is copyright. No part of it may be reproduced or transmitted in any form without the written permission of the publishers.
The publishers would like to thank The Essential Ingredient for props used in photography and Lumière, Surry Hills; Zinc Bar, Potts Point; and Café Zoe, Redfern, for use of their premises for photography.

To order books,
phone 136 116 (within Australia).
Send recipe enquiries to:
recipeenquiries@acpmagazines.com.au